Daddy, There's a Light in the Sky

An Illumination of Life Stories

Charles R. Twyman

authorHOUSE®

AuthorHouse™
1663 Liberty Drive
Bloomington, IN 47403
www.authorhouse.com
Phone: 1-800-839-8640

First published by AuthorHouse   7/14/2009

ISBN: 978-1-4389-8583-1 (e)
ISBN: 978-1-4389-8582-4 (sc)
ISBN: 978-1-4389-8581-7 (hc)

Printed in the United States of America
Bloomington, Indiana

This book is printed on acid-free paper.

To the memory of my mother and father,
and to
my wife Kay and my sister Alyce
and to all the others who have touched my life.

Preface

Rationale for Writing

My first thoughts were to write an autobiographical portrait. This presented a few problems in that I had delayed doing this for such a long time. Many of those persons who had shared my life had died and could no longer corroborate my material.

After much thought it came to me that though life is one continuous series of happenings; there are periods in life that are of far greater interest than others.

What then is a viable strategy for outlining and writing a book about one's life? First, with few exceptions, there is a novel in just about everyone's life. Note the fact that was stated or maybe I should say the idea offered is in fact a modification of a definitive statement. I noted that there are a few folk in this world whose life is so bland that they have no story to tell.

Well, I believe I have not one but many stories to tell. What is even of greater interest is that if it is God's will that I have another twenty or thirty years I'll have many more stories to tell. Every day presents a new scenario. Each day presents a new tune, a new set of lyrics, a new pallet of color.

So I now lay before you a series of life pallets; life lyrics; and life tunes. Each one a slice of my life not unlike other life stories and yet unique in that each slice is about me and

I am the only one who can attest to what I have seen, felt, smelled, tasted and heard.

"Oh?" you say, " What is so unique about being born, living and dying? Everyone does it." But as I noted earlier just about everyone has a story to tell. I know that I do and I've tested some of these stories out on a diverse group of people. I've seen young people look at me in disbelief and older folk nod their heads in agreement.

My experiences cover eight decades. Within each decade some interesting things happened that touched me. I wasn't always the central figure. Whatever took place with my mother, father, sister, uncles, aunts, cousins or friends and acquaintances impacted my life and made the ensuing stories possible.

Contents

Some Historical Stuff

There are many people in the world who have lived a full and exciting life. There are many more who have lived a dull and unexciting life. There are still others who have just lived their lives.

Most of us have no idea how exciting, dull or otherwise mundane our lives have been until someone asks us to tell about life as we know it. We tend to shy away from telling people about ourselves. We may offer a little bit but generally balk at getting down to the real nitty gritty details. Even those who write the so called kiss and tell revelations fail to reveal the real self. And how easy it is to tell about others. We then trust the reader to deduce our role in the story.

Certainly a neophyte writer such as me is going to try not to follow in the path of other autobiographical writers. Rather at this stage of writing the story of one's life there is an awesome pressure to tell it all. But, doesn't that fulfill the statement made by many listeners and readers that "that's more than I need to know."

Writing one's autobiography is a form of catharsis; a purging of one's soul, so to speak; a release from the agony of keeping long held secrets to protect others from revelation of sins or acts of goodness that they would prefer not be told. By what right does an autobiographer have to reveal others' secrets?

The writer of an autobiography must by all means protect the anonymity of others. But how does one protect one's parents, siblings, friends and acquaintances? After perusing the outlines for this endeavor it became patently clear that the autobiographer's primary task is to tell the story, the history, the good, and the ugly in such a way so as not to indict but rather weave a tapestry which the reader may view and interpret. The reader then has an option to see this tapestry from another point of view. The reader may view the tapestry just as the autobiographer wove it. Or, the reader may examine the tapestry and try to find where the thread broke, where it was knotted and in what direction it continues. The reader will get to know the characters and how they interact with each other and the autobiographer.

One must pledge to one's self to present as honest a picture as one's memory permits. Does this imply that there is no historical research done? By no means. However, if one cannot rely on one's memory then maybe the subject should be turned over to a biographer who in order to protect him/herself must research or look for corroborating evidence. Much of this evidence comes from the writings or audio pronouncements of the subject which in turn are corroborated by persons who knew the subject or had been impacted by the person.

Sometime ago I was invited to speak to a group of fifth grade students at a local elementary school. The occasion was a celebration of Black History Month. Their teacher invited me to come in, according to her because I had the distinction of being the first black appointed to a principalship in New Haven, Connecticut.

When I arrived at the classroom I noticed that the room was decorated with pictures of well known and famous black Americans. The teacher introduced me to the class and I spent about fifteen minutes talking to the students. During the course of my talk I pointed to pictures of Martin Luther

King, Thurgood Marshall, Constance Baker Motley, Adam Clayton Powell, W.C. Handy and Langston Hughes. I noted that I had either met or talked to or knew them. There was a collective exclamation from the group and I did as many do when bragging a bit, told little stories of my meeting these great people. I got carried away.

About two weeks following my visit I received a packet of letters from the class along with a "thank you" note from the teacher. I shared the kids' letters with my wife and we shared a few chuckles. I had been reading the letters aloud and then began to read one from a young male student who ended his letter in the following words. "I enjoyed your visit but did you <u>really know</u> all those people?"

My wife and I started to laugh and then I stopped and became sober. I thought about what the young man had asked. He knew that the persons whose pictures were on his classroom bulletin board were famous. He knew because he had been told by his teachers and by the books he had read. He knew because the radio, television and newspapers had told him so.

How does a ten year old boy reconcile himself to the reality that someone stood in front of him and his class and stated that he had met or knew not one but six very famous people? How does this information filter through the mind of a boy who has been exposed to lies or at best half truths most of his life? After all, I stood before this group and pronounced that I knew six famous people. I offered no proof. Why should I be taken seriously?

It was this realization that caused me to consider writing an autobiographical essay. I was later urged by a group of middle school students to finish a story that I had shared with them on a visit to their classroom. A group of high school students interviewed me last spring and some of them asked me to continue telling my story. My story is really a series of stories about my life. My story does involve others, some family, some friends, some colleagues, some acquaintances and lastly just some folks who have touched my life.

The Avenue

Historians claim that Dixwell Avenue derived its name from one of the three regicide judges who convicted King Charles and sentenced him to be executed.

Dixwell Avenue begins at the northern boundary of the downtown Yale University campus. People say that "The Avenue" was named after an English judge who together with two other judges named Whalley and Goffe had to flee England after sentencing King Charles to death. The judges, it is said, were pursued to the New Haven Colony and fled north and west and met atop a hill hiding in a cave. The routes taken by the three judges were eventually named Dixwell Avenue, Goffe Street and Whalley Avenue.

Interestingly, it was Dixwell Avenue which became the northern escape route for the sons and daughters of former slaves and refugees from the New York riots. The move to Dixwell Avenue began in the middle and late 1800's. Churches, social institutions and businesses were established. It was in this setting that Charles found himself in 1917 just at the beginning of the Great War. He was 16 at the time and had come to New Haven.

"The Avenue" was the center of commerce for the area. People of at least three racial groups lived and operated businesses on "The Avenue." There was a police station (Precinct No. 4) on the corner of Dixwell Avenue and Webster Street, a hotel was on Webster Street and a tea-room provided a social setting for some of the ladies who lived in the area. On Dixwell Avenue there were several restaurants, bakeries, two small department stores, a fish market, several meat markets (butchers), at least two fruit and vegetable stores, two Chinese laundries, a candy maker, three pharmacies two pool halls, two furniture stores, two doctors' offices, three dentists' offices, a dry goods store, an ice cream parlor, and three churches including one Russian Orthodox, one Congregational and one African-Methodist Episcopal Zion. All of this was contained in a 10 block corridor. Streets other than Webster which either began or ended at Dixwell were Lake Place, Eaton Street, Bristol Street, Foote Street, Gregory Street, Charles Street, Admiral Street, Henry Street, and Munson Street.

Colored people, as they were called in the 1920's, lived primarily on Eaton, Webster, Foote, and Gregory Streets. They of course lived on other streets in the area but very few north of Gregory.

The Avenue (Dixwell)
Circa 1938

The Beginning

From the time I was a little boy I was told the story about my grandfather who had been born in slavery. According to my Dad's younger brother, my Uncle Jack, my grandfather Ambrose was owned by a family named Wormsley. He later married my grandmother Cornelia who was owned by James Twyman.

For years my cousins and I heard this story and repeated it as gospel truth. But hold on!

Several years ago (1997), I received a telephone call from a woman who introduced herself as one Beatrice Twyman Cremeens. She asked that I indulge her because she wanted to know if my family was from Virginia. She had a noticeably soft southern accent though she said that she was living in Ohio.

There was something about this woman's voice that engendered trust. She stated that she had some information that might be of interest to me and my family if indeed we had our roots in Virginia and particularly in Madison County and the town of Orange. This was indeed where my Dad's family had established their home. This was where Dad and his brothers and sisters were born; the place where they played and worked. This was the place where my grandfather Ambrose was born into slavery. Oh yes, I certainly was interested in what this woman had to say.

Mrs. Cremeens began by saying "I hope that you will not be upset by what I'm about to say." Before I could respond she said, "I believe that my grandfather, James Twyman, owned your grandfather." You can imagine, without too much difficulty, the silence that ensued. When I finally gathered my wits about me, and when I had quickly told myself, "Stay cool," I responded, "Oh, this is quite a surprise."

I then went on to relate Uncle Jack's story to Mrs. Cremeens. I made certain that I told her about my grandfather's desire to take the name Twyman when he married my grandmother whom I had been led to believe was owned by some person named Twyman.

Mrs. Cremeens professed to know little of the details surrounding the ownership of one Ambrose Twyman.

She told me that her grandfather had set his slaves free in 1849. That information really stunned me. Again I had to pull myself together. Mrs. Cremeens proceeded to tell me that a book had been written by an attorney in Ohio who had researched the matter. She promised to send me a copy. She also said that she would put me in touch with her cousin, one John Morgan Twyman, who lived in California.

John Morgan Twyman called me about two weeks after my conversation with Mrs. Cremeens. I recall picking up the telephone and hearing a rather crisp voice saying, "This is John Morgan Twyman". I had anticipated the call since Mrs. Cremeens had established herself in my mind as a kind, honest and determined woman.

Mr. Twyman let me know up front that he was ninety-three years old and had made a fortune in real estate. He said that he had done rather extensive research into the Twyman family history. He also noted that James Twyman was indeed a courageous man. He told me of James Twyman's endeavors to set his slaves free. This man of courage traveled to Pennsylvania and Ohio to examine the social climate and thereby determined which place would be most amenable to having a group of blacks placed in their midst. His plan was to do this. But he knew that to do so without preparation could prove tragic.

I asked John Morgan Twyman if he knew why James Twyman undertook this courageous act. He was not knowledgeable about what motivated James Twyman. But we both agreed that it had to be a strong motivation, for the laws of Virginia were very harsh, regarding the freeing of slaves. If anyone has doubts about this I refer them to Judge Leon Higginbottom's book on slave laws in the south.

According to John Morgan Twyman, James Twyman met with the slaves that he owned and set forth a plan. That plan included giving the slaves a choice of where they wanted to settle. The choices were Pennsylvania or Ohio. The slaves chose Ohio. Once the decision was made James Twyman purchased land in Ohio. He purchased supplies to sustain the group for one year and placed funds in trust for them.

The slaves were gathered together by James Twyman. He then set out on the long journey to Ohio with forty-seven slaves and a group of armed men to protect the convoy of wagons through northern Virginia.

All of this was related to me by John Morgan Twyman. He also told me about the Twymans, who arrived in the Virginia colony in the late 1600's. This man knew a great deal about the Twyman family history. But, he knew little about the history of my family.

By now you are no doubt wondering why I recited John Morgan Twyman's historical journey. It was because it just further made it clear in my mind that the whole institution of slavery was a debilitating force that tore at the core of humanity. But James Twyman, for whatever reason, must have seen the inhumane nature of this institution. He took an action that sought to restore life to forty-seven human beings and indirectly had an impact on my life and the lives of countless others.

Getting back to Mrs. Cremeens, the woman who dropped into my life so unexpectedly, she had no way of knowing that I had begun inquiring about my family's origins when I was in high school. At this early stage in my life I wanted to know how I got to be Charles Robert Twyman. I used to listen to my classmates talking about their origins. The roots of their existence for the most part were in England, Ireland, Germany, Poland, Lithuania, and Italy.

My friend Ray had a grandmother who spoke German. Johnny's family spoke Italian as did Bobby's. Each of these friends and others that I knew had customs and foods that were distinctive. I could not seem to find my ties to another place.

Colored people could only refer to "down south." There were some exceptions of course. There was a group of people in New Haven from the West Indies. They came from various islands in the Caribbean, but, primarily from Nevis.

These people had immigrated to the United States. They came through the naturalization process. They came through the gateway to freedom – Ellis Island. West Indian people had pride in the fact that they shared common goals with Europeans. They came to the United States seeking a better way of life. Even though their ancestors had suffered much of the same dehumanizing treatment that my ancestors had, these people were free to travel and seek new lives. They at that time were British subjects and were recognized as such. They were sometimes referred to as being arrogant. No! Arrogant was not the correct descriptor for these wonderful people. They were rightfully proud and were not afraid to show it.

My mother was born in New Haven and lived next door to West Indian immigrants. She became friends with the family. She was very close with one of the daughters, who was a gifted musician. My mother had been gifted with a beautiful voice which she utilized in the church choir of which her friend was the organist. My mother learned early of the dedication her West Indian neighbors had in educating their children. They were fully engrossed in family and work. Their goal was to succeed in America and they knew that hard work and a focus on the goal of becoming full citizens was essential.

My mother's family was no less dedicated to those same goals. Her folks had an interesting background. Her father, a Virginian, moved north to New Jersey in the 1870's. There he met and married a young woman who was of mixed African and Italian background. They had eight children (Jake, Katherine, Mary, Major, Louise, William, Jenny and Arthur). My mother's father worked on oyster boats before moving north. He worked on the Chesapeake Bay sailing out of Accomack, Virginia. It has been reported that he was on a boat that docked in Cape May, New Jersey. He left the boat and worked his way north to New Brunswick where he met his wife.

His wife's grandfather was an Italian seaman who married a slave woman, who, according to family lore he purchased and married. They had four children. Sabina was one of the daughters. She had several children one of whom was Katherine who married my mother's father.

Now if this begins to sound like "the begets and begots", it is. I found it suits the purpose of this work to not go beyond the boundaries of the knowledge of my family. This is all they ever told me about that branch of my family. So goes the oral history bit. I did find the name of the Italian, but again there is a question about the spelling. My aunt Katherine spelled it Carrelli, my mother spelled it Corelli. Now I believe my mother preferred Corelli because it was the name of a famous Italian composer of symphonic music. Mother studied music and I'm certain this had some influence on her preferred spelling.

But enough of this, I have established the roots of my existence and thus have plotted the paths of my 320 plus seasons on this earth.

My time on earth began early in the morning of June 28, 1922.

June 27, 1922

He returned from his job as a porter in a downtown department store passing through the crowded avenue waving to acquaintances, and cavalierly tipping his cap to an occasional lady. He smiled self consciously when Doc the pharmacist said, "When's the baby due Charlie?" "Pretty soon now I guess Doc." "I sure hope so," he thought. His older brothers had not told him what to expect during this last month of Nick's pregnancy. They both had kids, but they never told him how touchy a woman gets during the last month. "Damn," he thought. "I can't do a damn thing right."

Charles thought about how difficult it had been for him to move from the comfort of the private boy's preparatory school to the hustle bustle of the city. He thought about the similarity of the boys' school he had just left to the one where his father worked in Virginia. He remembered how his father had threatened to horsewhip him and his younger brother Jack if they failed to learn something each day. With a smile he recalled listening to the students and teachers talking as they passed by.

A couple passing Charles silently wondered if Charles had been drinking because he started to chuckle audibly just as they passed each other while crossing Dixwell Avenue. The rattle of a passing trolley car drowned out an even louder guffaw as Charles thought about how he had wheedled book knowledge out of the teachers and students.

The rattle of the trolley jolted him from his thoughts of Virginia and Woodbury Forest School. It returned him to the reality of where he was at that moment. The moment was vividly etched in his olfactory senses when he realized that he had just stepped into a pile of fresh horse manure. Mr. Wiley's horse had just passed and left the remains of his last meal on the pavement.

Charles stopped at the curb and set to work scraping the horse manure from his shoe. As he bent over engrossed in his task he heard someone comment, "Look at ole Charlie – Just stepped in some good luck!" "Good luck," thought Charles. "If I take any of it home I'll probably have to sleep outside!" He proceeded north on Dixwell Avenue until he got to Henry Street. He stopped and looked in the window of Rosenberg's Furniture and Appliance store. "Guess I'd better start thinking about some new furniture. Nick and I'll be needing a new bed and the baby will need a crib. Damn! How?"

Just as he decided to turn the corner into Henry Street he remembered that he had promised to bring home some chops for dinner. That meant he had to walk all the way back to Bristol Street, five blocks. "Oh damn it anyhow!" he exclaimed. "Why didn't I think of it ten minutes ago? Oh well!" As he headed down the avenue he spotted Ol' Comrade staggering across the avenue and holding up his hands to halt Doc Porter's new Model T Ford. Everyone nearby nearly doubled up with laughter when Doc stopped and Ol' Comrade did a perfect about face and crossed the street again, stopping traffic coming in the opposite direction. This included two trolley cars. As trolley bells clanged and horns blew, Comrade stopped again, did a perfect left face and began marching down Dixwell Avenue with a parade of automobiles and trolley cars rolling ever so slowly behind him.

The parade proceeded down Dixwell Avenue for one block until it reached the intersection at Webster Street when a tall ruddy faced police officer stepped off the curb and confronted Comrade, saluted him and said, "Beggin' your pardon Sergeant, but may I have a word with you?" Comrade smartly saluted the police officer and replied, "As soon as I've dismissed my troops." He then turned and addressing the nearest automobile yelled "Company Halt!! Company Dismissed! He then turned to the policeman and said "At your service – sir!"

There was a loud cheer from all four corners of the intersection. The sound of trolley bells and Model T's again permeated the air and Charles found himself a block past his destination because he too had joined Comrade's parade. He felt very sad as he saw the policeman escort Comrade up the stairs of Precinct 4. He wondered what would happen once Comrade got inside the station house and Sergeant Henry took charge. Charles had heard that Sergeant Henry was a very tough man. As he stood there on the corner big Bill Porter came up and said, "Whadda ya say there boy?" Charles turned to face Big Bill and said, "I was just wondering what's going to happen to Comrade when they get him inside there?"

Big Bill let a big smile gradually spread over his broad, light complexioned face and quietly rumbled, "Just wait out here a few minutes boy – That ol' Irishman in there knows how to deal with Comrade. Just wait and watch."

Charles thought, "Wait and watch what? I don't have time to be standin' out here on the corner. Hell! I don't even know Ol' Comrade!" Then he said to Big Bill, "Somebody ought to talk to Ol' Comrade, that man's been actin' crazy ever since I came to this town."

Bill reacted most strangely. He grabbed Charles by the arm, not roughly, but certainly quite firmly. Charles' first reaction was to jerk his arm away but something stayed that action. He turned so that he was fully facing Big Bill then said, "Did I say something wrong?" "Nah, it wasn't something you said, it was more who you were. Believe it or not I'll bet you Ol' Comrade is about two, no more than three years older than you." Bill loosened his grip on Charles' arm and sighed.

"How old are you anyway? I remember when you first came here from Poughkeepsie with your brothers. You couldn't have been more than eighteen." "Sixteen," Charles interjected. "Sixteen" said Big Bill reflecting. He then said, "That was six years ago." "Seven," Charles again interjected. "That makes you ..." "Twenty-three," said Charles.

"Well Ol' Comrade is just twenty-six. He served Uncle Sam in France in "17" and "18". I served with him and let me tell you he was one hell of a soldier. We were in Company G, 2nd Battalion, 372 Regiment. Oh man was he a soldier! I remember when they sent us to Camp Dix in New Jersey. Most of us were really scared half to death. But Ol' Comrade – now he was something else. Why in less than a month he was a Sergeant. In fact he was my Sergeant. And believe me boy, I say that proudly."

Just as Big Bill caught his breath to continue Ol' Comrade appeared on the steps of the station house. He wasn't bloody or bruised. His clothes which had been in dishabille were straightened. His hair was combed and he walked down the steps without hesitation with his head held high.

Charles turned and looked at Big Bill a question framed on his face. "Wha". Before he could complete the word Big Bill said "Ol' Comrade saved Sergeant Henry's brother's life down at Camp Dix. Seems like there was some name calling one day and a few of them Irish jumped one of the guys in Company A. Well those Negroes in Co. A were from Boston and the ones who did the name calling and berating were Irish from New York. Well, those boys from Boston waited until night and began to pick those Irishmen off one by one.

Charles said, "You mean they shot 'em?" "Naw they whipped their asses real good," exclaimed Big Bill. Charles just nodded his head and looked at Big Bill waiting to hear the rest of the story.

Big Bill sensing Charles" interest went on. "Well, they had whipped about five of those Paddy asses when they came on a little narrow assed soldier. One of the Company A guys grabbed him and pushed him to the ground. Well he hardly touches the ground and he's up swinging like a crazy damn fool. He grabbed a broken tree limb and started swinging. All of a sudden the boys in Company A realize this Irishman ain't going to lie down and play dead like the others.

Well sir! That damn Irishman had knocked down four of them bully Negroes when one of 'em pulls out a knife. The Irishman saw the damn knife and instead of him running away he runs over to the guy with the knife and says "C'mon I'll fight you with or without the knife. The guy from Company A starts swinging that knife and Josh – that's Ol' Comrade's real name – appears and yells. "Hey Slick put that knife down before you hurt somebody!" The guy from Company A didn't pay any heed to Josh and keeps swinging that knife back and forth, back and forth.

Before anybody knows it Josh walks up beside the Negro with the knife and kicks him in the balls. Well sir, he lets out a howl but holds onto the knife, grabs the Irishman and starts slicing. There was blood everywhere. If you think that Irishman ran away, guess again. He punched that son of a bitch about ten times. But now that Negro's gone crazy. He starts yellin' and cryin' an all kinds of funny things. Only there wasn't nothin' funny.

Well…Ol' Josh comes up behind the son of bitch and this time he's got a piece of tree limb… He hit that bully once and down he went. Not a sound out him. He just went down.

Now the Irishman, he just stood there lookin' like somebody painted his shirt red. Josh walks over and says 'C'mon, I'll take you to the medic.'

Would you believe that damn thick Irishman looks Josh in the eye and says 'Don't come near me you black bastard.'

Josh didn't say a word he just put the stick down, walked over to the Irishman hit him right on the chin. The Irishman was out cold when he hit the ground. Josh picked him up and took him to the medic."

Charles had been listening to this recital with great interest all the while thinking about what Reverend McCoy had said last Sunday about how colored soldiers were being treated by white people in the South. He thought to himself. "White folks up here aren't much different from down home. Fact is, maybe they're more honest down there than up here. At least I knew down there that white people and colored people didn't get along and so they just stayed on their own side of the road. Heck they knew Poppa would shoot anybody colored or white, who set foot on his land intending to do harm to any of his family. So nobody ever set foot on the land with that in mind."

Poppa was a horseman. That is he knew horses better than anyone else living around the mill.

Old Doc, the man Poppa drove for, used to tell everybody that he not only had a coachman but a trainer, a veterinarian and a damn smart nigger.

Poppa used to tell people that Old Doc was a mean, cantankerous, nigger hating old man. But, he was a good doctor and he knew horses so that made him special.

Old Doc's parents had been slave owners and owned Momma's parents. Though Poppa told folks that Old Doc was mean, he really respected the old man because that man respected him and his wife. Further more he delivered all the kids except Otha. Shucks all the other families around the grist mill were born without any doctor being around. Most of the time there wasn't even a mid-wife. Lots of kids died back then.

The thought of kids dying brought a shudder to Charles' body when he thought about the impending birth of his first child. He also remembered that he had to take home a package of lamb chops for Nick.

With this thought in mind he turned and headed back up the avenue away from the butcher from whom he intended to purchase the chops. When he got to Eisles Market, a market that serviced the rich, he stopped just before entering and felt his pocket to be sure he had enough money to make the purchase. He walked into the store and immediately sensed something amiss. Looking around he noticed a tall stately woman who without doubt was rich. Standing next to her was another woman who was wearing a maid's uniform. Charles noticed that the maid was crying and holding a handkerchief to her face. When she lowered the handkerchief he recognized her as a member of his church. He tipped his cap and started toward her but she caught his eye and signaled him to stop.

Somewhat puzzled Charles stopped in his tracks and walked over to the butcher. "Well, what do you want?" asked the straw hatted butcher. "I want $1.00 worth of lamb chops." The butcher smiled and went into the icebox and came out with a piece of meat which he began to work on. He worked first with the knife, then with saw and finally with the cleaver. He placed four pieces of meat on the scale and said. That will be exactly $1.20. Charles reached into his pocket, took out a dollar bill and a quarter, handed it to the butcher and stood waiting for his change.

The butcher went to the cash drawer, placed the money in it, returned and handed Charles his package. Charles started for the door and then remembered that he had a nickel's change due. He turned and said to the butcher, "You forgot my change."

A smile slowly spread over the butcher's face and he beckoned to Charles. When Charles was standing close the butcher hissed, "What are you trying to do nigger?" Are you trying to embarrass me in front of my customer?"

Charles' first reaction was shock but quickly turned to anger. Without thinking he reached for the butcher who jumped back from the counter, slipped on the sawdust covered floor and fell in a heap next to the scrap barrel. He began to holler as he hit the floor. "Call the police. That nigger just hit me!"

Charles wanted to laugh but swallowed that inclination when he saw the expression on the faces of the other butcher and the rich woman customer. The woman's maid turned toward Charles and whispered, "You better get out of here before the cops come." She turned toward her mistress and said, "M'am that man wasn't hit, he just fell trying to get away. I saw the whole thing."

Her mistress grunted, "So did I. I also heard what he called that boy." She then turned and walked over to the owner of the market and suggested that he take care of her order immediately. The owner who was also a butcher yelled to his employee, "Get up and get to work!"

"But what about the police!" exclaimed the butcher?

"Shut up and get Mrs. Barnes' order taken care of," the owner yelled.

Charles stood for a moment then quietly asked, "Can I have my change?"

The store owner looked at Charles, rolled his eyes heavenward and said, "How much do I owe you?" Charles said, "Five cents." The owner reached into his pocket took out a nickel and handed it to Charles.

Charles started toward the door then turned and said, "Thank you."

As he crossed the Avenue heading toward home Charles thought about the incident and how close he had come to having to explain to a policemen what had happened. "Shucks," he thought, "I didn't do anything except ask for my change and that fat German called me a nigger. I should have hit him with my fist. He would 've had something to complain about then."

He began to wonder why that rich white woman spoke up for him. He knew the maid. But she had told him to run away when he had done nothing. Strange.

When he arrived in front of the large double porch house on Orchard Street he looked up to the third floor where he and his wife Louise lived. The windows were open and he could see her hand waving a greeting to him.

He walked around to the back of the house and went up the three flights of stairs. As he got to the top the door opened and there stood Louise whom he fondly called Nick.

Louise looked at Charles and smiled warmly then pointed to her protruding stomach and said, "This child has been raising a fuss all day. I think she's ready to be born.

Charles laughed and said, "Hello! I'm home! How are you feeling? And that's a boy in there not a girl!"

She slapped him playfully then said, "My sister Katie came by and brought us some eggs from Pop's chickens. She said she and John would come by tomorrow."

"On Wednesday? How's John going to do that? Doesn't he have to work?" Charles wasn't too fond of John and really didn't like being around him. The only thing that seemed to interest John was money. It seemed that every time John did something he always attached a dollar and cents value to it. He asked Charles one day not too long ago, "How much is the baby going to cost you?"

Up to that point Charles hadn't even given thought to how much a baby cost. Back home when his brother Jack and sister Martha were born, his mother's cousin Cindy came by and Poppa's Aunt Missouri stopped in and the next thing he knew he had a younger brother and another sister. Momma and Poppa never talked about how much a baby cost, and old Doc, never charged Poppa any money.

Though he hated to admit it John had caused him to wonder just how much this baby was going to cost. Already he and Nick had had to leave their rent free apartment in Milford because the school didn't want a pregnant maid around the boys. Then he had to find a rent he thought he could afford. He also had to get some furniture. "Yeah! I guess a baby is kind of expensive," he thought.

He then thought about something that brought a smile to his face. Kate and John had been married since 1914 and they didn't yet have any kids. Yeah, John didn't have any kids that he could brag about. He also didn't have to contend with all the problems that came along with starting a family.

"Say, Nick! How does John get so much time off anyhow?" Louise shuffled slowly across the kitchen and picked up the package of chops. She opened the package and a slow smile spread across her face. Turning to her husband she said, "Four chops are just about enough for me – What are you planning to have for dinner?"

Charles returned the smile and quickly replied "A bit of rump steak – Your rump if you don't get those chops cooked real soon!"

Louise began to laugh and her whole body shook. Suddenly the laugh turned to a loud wail and she grasped the edge of the sink. "I think the baby's coming, "she gasped.

Charles stood transfixed. He let his mouth gape, his eyes popped, he began to tremble. He mumbled something that sounded like – "Baby can't come right now." Louise gained control of herself and said in a rather sharp tone, "Go get the doctor! Charles, go get the doctor!"

Charles started to the door and then turned back. "Nick," he shouted "What is that doctor's name anyhow?"

Louise exasperatedly replied, "Dr. Ford". She then added, "Hurry up!!"

Charles stood there a minute and then bolted out the door and down the stairs. When he got to the front door he opened it and ran across the front porch, jumped the three steps to the ground and started running down Orchard Street. He passed a neighbor, Mrs. Pughsley and shouted "The baby's coming!" Poor Mrs. Pughsley didn't quite hear Charles and thought rather indignantly, "What does he mean, "Hello Baby! Humph. He has some nerve. Why I'm old enough to be his mother." Just as she turned to tell him just that, she noticed that Charles had stopped in the middle of the street apparently in some confusion.

Charles turned and started back toward Mrs. Pughsley. This time she was ready and she waited for him, preparing to give him a piece of her mind. Suddenly she noted that Charles had a perplexed look on his face and she wondered what was bothering him.

Just as she prepared to speak, Charles said, "M'am can you help me? My wife is about to have a baby and I've got to get the doctor and there's nobody with her. M'am could you…" Before he could finish the sentence Mrs. Pughsley asked, "Who is your doctor?"

Charles replied "Dr. Ford." Mrs. Pughsley said to Charles. "You go home and stay with your wife and I'll go into my house and telephone Dr. Ford. Now you hurry home!!"

Charles turned and ran back to his house, which was about four houses from Mrs. Pughsley's, and ran up the three flights of stairs. When he walked in the apartment he was shocked not to see Louise. He called out "Nick! Nick, where are you?" He heard her voice coming from the bedroom. She said, "I'm in here bring the doctor in."

Charles walked to the bedroom door, looked in and saw Louise sitting on the side of the bed. She looked up at him expectantly.

"Where is the doctor?" she asked. Charles couldn't at that moment remember Mrs. Pughsley's name. He hesitated for a moment.

"Where is the doctor Charles?" This time Louise's voice was edgy.

Charles attempting to ease the tension a little said "The lady down the street is going to telephone Dr. Ford."

"What lady Charles? Charles, what lady? I need the doctor right now!!! Charles, what lady?"

Charles could not think of the woman's name and now began to have some doubt about the wisdom of having someone do what he had set out to do. Just then he heard a knock on the door and he turned to go and open it when Louise again asked, "What lady Charles? Charles answer me! What lady?"

Charles prayed that the knock on the door was the doctor. He jerked the door open. It was not the doctor. It was Mrs. Pughsley and another woman whom he did not know. He looked at Mrs. Pughsley and anxiously asked "Where's the doctor?"

Mrs. Pughsley replied, "Coming." She then asked "Where is your wife?" Before Charles could reply the woman with Mrs. Pughsley swept by Charles and started toward the bedroom. Charles started to protest but one look from the woman froze the words on his lips.

Mrs. Pughsley said to Charles" Put a big pot of water on the stove to boil!" She then said "Where do you keep your sheets?"

Charles wanted to go to the bedroom to see how Louise was doing. But as soon as he looked in the direction of the bedroom Mrs. Pughsley said, "Young man put that water on right now!"

There was something about Mrs. Pughsley that did not encourage anyone to not follow her commands. Just as Charles put the water on the stove he heard Louise scream. He started toward the bedroom. Mrs. Pughsley said "Young man, get those sheets for me right away."

As Charles turned to go to the closet to get the sheets another knock sounded at the door.

Dr. Ford was a young woman. She was quite tall and very attractive. She stood at the door and smiled at Charles. "Where is Louise, Charles? I received a call from one of your neighbors who said that the baby was on the way." Just at that moment Louise let out another yelp. Charles pulled the doctor into the house and propelled her in the direction of the bedroom.

When Louise saw the doctor she exclaimed "I didn't believe you'd get here in time! Oh, I'm so glad to see you!" Dr. Ford gave Louise a reassuring hug and then told the two women to put some blankets and a sheet on the kitchen table. She then called to Charles and told him to move the table to the center of the room under the light.

The doctor then walked out of the bedroom and told Charles to walk downstairs and sit down until she called him. Charles started to protest but Mrs. Pughsley said, "You go ahead now. Everything is going to be fine." There was something in her smile that reminded him of his mother when she had something special for supper which she wanted to keep as a surprise. He started down the stairs slowly feeling that something really good was about to happen.

June 28th

When she was a little girl about eight years old Louise's mother died. She died shortly after Arthur was born. Louise somehow knew that her mother was going to die. She dreamed about it twice. Once when she was five and then again just before it happened.

This afternoon as she lay on the bed waiting for the doctor she again lapsed into a state closely akin to sleep and again she dreamed. She started to murmur to her mother who was standing at the foot of the bed. She heard her say, "The baby is going to be fine and he'll grow tall and strong."

Louise called out, "Momma it's got to be a girl!" she felt the soothing cool dampness of the towel as it was placed on her head. She awakened and looked into the face of Mrs. Pughsley.

Mrs. Pughsley had a strange look on her face but when Louise looked at her questioningly a smile, gently passed across Mrs. Pughsley's face. Louise smiled back and said "I was dreaming that my mother was here. "Mrs. Pughsley nodded and smiled and thought to herself." How can anyone dream with their eyes wide open?"

"How do you feel child, "asked Mrs. Pughsley in her best motherly tone. Louise replied, "I'm hurting just awful. Where is Charles with the doctor?" "Don't worry child the doctor is right here and your husband is just fine."

He sure is a fine looking young man said Mrs. Pughsley's friend who up to this point had just been standing beside the bed. Louise looked up at the woman questioningly. She didn't recognize her and was about to say so when the baby gave her a reminder as to why she was lying on the bed. "Oh my God!" screamed Louise and reached over and grabbed Mrs. Pughsley's friend pulling her off balance. The woman slipped and fell in an undignified heap on her rather plentiful bottom. Both the doctor and Mrs. Pughsley jerked their heads around to see what the commotion was about. Mrs. Pughsley's friend was sitting on the floor legs akimbo and a surprised look on her face.

Time seemed to go by very rapidly and night soon came. The baby decided not to make an appearance until about one o'clock in the morning. It seemed to be a sign that the baby was introduced to this world on a kitchen table.

Charles Robert was a loud arrival. His cries awakened his father who had fallen asleep in a chair on the back steps three flights down. Charles could not believe he heard a baby cry and he jerked around peering into the darkness of the night. He then smiled and went up the stairs to the third floor apartment which was now bright with light. He walked in and was met by a smiling Mrs. Pughsley, her friend and Dr. Ford. Charles looked around for Louise and didn't see her. He stood there sort of dumbfounded when he heard a baby's cry coming from the bedroom. He turned and walked in. The three women were right behind him each one giggling as they watched him standing there mouth agape seemingly not knowing what to do. Go forward? Back up?

Louise finally spoke and said, "Come here and hold this hungry boy." Charles said, "Boy?" "Yes!!!" chorused the doctor, Mrs. Pughsley and friend, "a bouncing boy." The doctor said, "Charles he is healthy. He woke up the world with his birth cry and wanted to suckle right away." Mrs. Pughsley said,

"He was born on a kitchen table and must think he should be fed right away."

Charles reached down and picked up the baby and said, "Thank you Lord and thank you Nick."

Well that, with a few embellishments, is how I arrived here more than eighty summers ago. I arrived naked and hungry and surrounded by women.

Packing

It was three weeks before Christmas. Things were hectic at the house. All of the dishes and glasses were being wrapped in newspaper and being placed in the large boxes that Charles had brought from the store. The baby was sitting up in a large laundry basket seemingly noticing everything that was happening.

Louise looked over at the baby and commented to her sister Catherine, "Katie, it sure doesn't seem like that little rascal has been here six months. I've been so busy trying to get things ready to move that I've hardly had time to think. If it wasn't for Amelia helping the way she had I don't know what I would have done."

Catherine didn't look up from her wrapping and said, "Um, I guess she's been some help but my God! Why did you two decide to take that child? What with a new baby. I can't understand it. After all it's not like you two have a lot of money and you sure don't have any extra time. But, I guess you're right about her helping out. She does well for a seven year old."

"You know that she's a very bright child and Charles and I expect great things of her. Who knows, she could grow to be a nurse like Laura Belle or even a doctor like Doctor Ford." Louise added, "She also is a talented little artist." "Uh huh," Katie grunted. She added her usual final line. "Who's going to pay for all of that? It costs a lot of money to go to college." Louise said, "Yes, but our brother Major got into Howard and he didn't have any money.

"You're right, "Katie replied. "Remember how we all put our nickels and dimes together to send him eating money?" "But who's going to do that for Amelia?"

There was a loud knock at the door. Both women jumped instinctively because their minds had not been focused on anything but packing and talking.

Louise called out, "Who is it?" A male voice, not familiar to her, responded. "It's me, Gillie" Louise looked at Katie questioningly.

Katie yelled, "Gillie? How'd you find me here?" "Billy told me where you were." Katie laughed and said to Louise, "Gillie's my number man." Louise said, "You mean a gambling, hustler man, don't you?" Katie smiled and said, "You're right but he pays twenty dollars for a two cent play and he don't take any for himself."

Louise said, "Charles told me that Bolito is run by some of those slick Cubans out of New York and that they don't take no stuff from nobody. Is that Gillie one of them?"

Katie laughed and said "Gillie's from Delaware. Ain't no Cubans down there! He came up here about twenty years ago with John. In fact, him and John used to work together."

Louise said, "Birds of a feather."

Katie cut her off saying "Just hold on there John is my husband and he's fed half my family from what he brings home from down at Yale. I don't hear no complaints about the extra food."

"Oh shut up Katie," Louise spat out. "I wasn't saying anything bad about John – even though" and her voice trailed off.

Both realized that Gillie was standing there taking it all in with a half smile on his moon-like continence. He said, "Miz Kate what numbers do you want today?" Katie gazed up at the ceiling and then at the cupboard that she and Louise had been working on and said, "Ten, twelve, fifteen, six and five; two cents each. That will be a dime, right?"

"Yes'm" Gillie said. "You came close yesterday." He held out his hand as Katie searched her bag for a dime. His hand closed around the money and he dropped it into a little black purse, fat with pennies, nickels and dimes. Gillie started toward the door and turned and said to Louise. "Charlie's right – them Cubans don't take no stuff. Cut your throat if you steal anything from them – even ten cents. But they pay off if you hit the numbers. See you ladies. Good day!"

With Gillie gone the two sisters resumed their tasks of wrapping and packing.

Chick's Booze Run

My mother had several brothers all of whom she loved dearly. Major had gone to college and studied dentistry. He was probably Mom's favorite and the one she wanted me to grow up to be most like. But Uncle Major didn't live in New Haven. And though I really wanted to be as great as Uncle Major in all endeavors, the one who had the greatest influence on my life was Uncle Chick.

Uncle Chick also idolized his older brother Major and patterned his early life after him. Major was an outstanding athlete. Some have even likened him to the famous Native American Jim Thorpe. Major excelled in football, basketball, baseball, hockey and track.

Chick was a real great athlete especially in football, basketball and baseball. He lettered in all three sports and received a scholarship to Lincoln University as a result.

But there was much more to Chick's life than sports. Chick was an adventurous young man who, like many his age, had no fear of any man.

This of course did not mean that he had no fear. He had, very much as his older sisters and brothers, been exposed to the Baptist Church quite early in his life. The result – a healthy fear of God. Well maybe a healthy fear of being caught doing wrong.

One of the stories told within the family circle was about how Chick avoided being caught doing something wrong.

Chick spent his summer as a driver for a dairy. He used to deliver large twenty gallon cans of milk to restaurants, bakeries, and to the railroad dining cars. His duties consisted of delivery of full cans and picking up the empty cans.

Chick's brother-in-law, my Uncle John, was the chef and manager of one of Chick's stops. The year was 1926 during the height of prohibition.

Now one must understand that Uncle John was Aunt Katie's husband. This is significant because Aunt Katie was Uncle Chick's oldest sister, and she was the person to whom all the younger children looked up to, especially Chick. So if Katie's husband John directed Chick to do something – he did it – without question.

Having gotten that concept out of the way, let's get back to Chick's job as a milk delivery man.

Uncle John in his role as chef and manager of one of the university's most prestigious secret societies was also the procurer of alcoholic beverages for his employer. Procuring bootleg booze was no problem. But John, who did not want to chance passing on some poisonous booze to his employers, devised a scheme that would provide high quality distilled rye whiskey to them.

The scheme was simple and involved a few friends and his young brother-in-law Chick.

Uncle John's friends Clarence and Lloyd were dining car waiters. Both worked for the railway company who ran between Washington, D.C. and Montreal, Canada. They had been friends and working partners for many years. In fact, they met while attending college in Washington, D.C. Both had majored in chemistry. This fact fit into Uncle John's scheme to provide quality booze to his clients.

The scheme as noted above was simple. It required Chick to deliver two twenty gallon cans of milk to a railroad stop about fifteen miles from New Haven. This stop was not for passengers but only for ice and other dining car supplies. He was also required to pick up two empty milk cans. Simple, right? Well things happen.

Uncle John's plan was for Chick to drop off two containers of milk and to pick up two containers that Clarence and Lloyd would place on the platform. These two containers of course were not empty but contained several quarts of good Canadian rye whiskey.

Chick usually got to the stop a few minutes before the train and he unloaded his milk cans. He then waited for Clarence and Lloyd to come in on the train. They usually passed the few minutes joking about girls and talking about family. Lloyd usually helped Chick load the two supposedly empty cans onto Chick's truck. Chick then passed on an envelope to Lloyd. Chick would then drive off to New Haven with his cargo to deliver to Uncle John.

One day Chick was delayed and missed seeing Clarence and Lloyd. However when he arrived there were three "empty" milk cans sitting in the usual place on the platform. Chick went about his usual routine except dropping off full milk cans. After all he reasoned the milk would spoil. So he loaded the "empty" cans onto the truck.

He started the truck and drove toward the road. Just as he reached the entry to the road a black touring car turned into the entry to the rail loading platform. He was somewhat surprised since no passengers either embarked or debarked from the train at this place.

Chick started down Route 1 – the Boston Post Road – toward New Haven. He had gone no more than a mile when he heard the honking of a car horn accompanied by lights flashing behind him. Looking back he discerned the black touring car riding right on his tail. Since the road had only two lanes Chick slowed the truck and pulled over so that the touring car might pass.

Chick thought the people in the car might be trying to catch the train in New Haven having discovered that the train did not pick up or discharge passengers at the supply platform. He was more than surprised when the car pulled abreast and he looked down to see a man wearing a cap pointing a pistol at him.

As mentioned earlier, Chick feared no man. He immediately pushed his foot down on the clutch put the gear shift lever into second gear. He turned the wheel so the truck was heading directly at the side of the car. The car swerved into the opposite lane. Chick pressed the accelerator to the floor and off he went down Route 1 leaving behind a shower of gravel and dust.

Racing through Chick's mind was the thought that the police were going to arrest him for carrying illegal liquor. It never dawned on him that it might be someone other than the police. But that thought soon left him when he heard a loud bang and discovered that he was being fired on by someone with a shotgun.

Chick had never driven the truck at any speed over thirty miles per hour. The car had no problem keeping up with the truck at that speed. Chick however decided to push the truck to its limit. He had no idea how fast he was driving. He had one thing in mind. That was simply, "Don't get caught!"

Uncle John had warned Chick to be careful and not to attract attention to himself or the truck. He also cautioned Chick to always be on time to meet the train, take care of the transfer and to get back on the road. He had also warned Chick not to stop for anyone.

The sight of the pistol and the sound of the shotgun precluded any idea of stopping. Chick was determined not to be caught by the police or anyone else. He shuddered at the thought of being exposed as a rum runner. This thought motivated him to go even faster.

As he sped down the Post Road he wondered what he would do when he got to town. He reasoned that if he was being chased by the police he would surely be caught when he got into the city.

At this moment he noted that he was about to cross the bridge leading into town. Just as he entered the bridge the safety gate went down behind him. He looked back just in time to see the black touring car screech to a halt. The gate had come down just in front of the car.

Chick looked heavenward and shouted out "Thank you Jesus." He then continued on into town never once looking back until he reached his destination on the Yale campus.

Chick backed the truck across the sidewalk to the stairs leading down to the kitchen area of the secret society building. He went down the stairs and pulled the bell cord.

Within a few minutes the door opened and Uncle John looked out and exclaimed, "What in the name of heaven happened to you?" Chick who sometimes stammered finally got the words "Almost got killed," out of his mouth. John asked, "What happened?" Chick said, "Got shot at." "What? By who?" queried John. "Don't know!" said Chick. He then said "Let's unload the cans."

John and Chick unloaded the milk first and then the booze. John stopped at the second can but Chick said "That one's ours too." Now John looked at Chick and said, "You know we only get two cans on each delivery. Chick said, "Well this time there were three cans at the siding and I loaded all of them. John took the tops from the three cans and sniffed them. Two of them had the pungent odor of rye whiskey. The third can had a smoky odor which John immediately identified as scotch whiskey.

"Scotch whiskey!" exclaimed John. "What in the name of heaven did you do boy?" Chick resented being called boy by his brother-in-law. His sister Kate always called him boy. But this was different. His first inclination was to snap back at John. He realized that he must have done something to upset John.

John looking worried finally made clear to Chick what the problem was. He said to Chick, "This can belongs to the Italian guy they call the Stinger. They say he belongs to a gang."

What Uncle John was explaining to Chick was that somehow Chick had picked up some booze that belonged to a gang of New Haven Italian bootleggers. He knew that these people did not tolerate any interference with their business. The fact that shots had been fired at Chick attested to that.

Chick's response was typical of a young fearless man of that period. "Well, let's just give it back to them."

John looked up and with a smile said, "Why not?" So he placed the top back on the can of scotch whiskey, placed it back on the truck and got in the passenger seat. He turned to Chick and said "C'mon boy we've got a delivery to make."

Chick drove the truck out onto the street and started toward Chapel Street. He turned into Orchard Street and went over to Goffe. He turned right onto Goffe and went three blocks to Webster. When he got to the corner of Webster and Goffe, John said, "Stop here," and got down from the passenger seat, went over to the door of a building with a sign reading Campania Club. He knocked and called out – "Milk delivery for Mr. Stinger."

Uncle John and Uncle Chick then unloaded the milk can to the sidewalk, climbed into the truck and drove off. As they drove off several young men emerged from the club and one of them lifted the cover from the can, sniffed, returned the cover and uttered, "Fuckin' smart mulyams." He then directed the other young men to move the can into the club.

The Move

It took awhile before Louise and Charles were ready to move from their third floor apartment. Their new apartment was a first floor two bedroom apartment in a two family house. The second floor apartment was occupied by the owners of the house.

The owners were a childless couple who originally came from New York City. The husband was a chef for the Pullman Company. He worked on private rail cars for very influential persons who leased the private cars for extended periods of time. His wife was a fair complexioned woman who was a gentle sweet person who loved babies.

Louise and Charles knew this wonderful couple from church. Both Charles and Louise were members of the choir. Louise was a soloist and part of the alto section. Charles was a bass and joined with Aaron and Robert to form a powerful bass section. All of the ladies in the congregation quivered a little when the three men came down the center aisle of the church singing along with the other choir members.

One of the ladies in the congregation confided to a friend that when those three men processed down the aisle she could actually feel the vibrations from the low notes down to her toes. Of course her confidant acted properly shocked. However she never admitted that she too felt similarly somewhere between her waist and her toes. Secretly they both coveted the three basso profundos.

But getting back to the owners of the house who were extraordinary people. He was very dark complexioned, bald on top of his head, and fine grey hair on the sides of his head. One feature that stood out was his piercing blue eyes. He had a closely trimmed moustache, thin lips and high cheek bones. He dressed conservatively. He wore starched collars and cuffs on his shirts. Most of the time he wore a dark blue suit with a vest and carried a gold pocket watch attached to a rather thick gold chain. He loved his watch and chain. They were gifts from his wife.

His wife was a heavy set woman with a beautiful face with long grey hair. She seemed to always have a smile on her face. She was from upstate New York one of two daughters of a farmer. She and her sister had never seen a real black man before Willis came along. Needless to say they were mesmerized by this dapper railroad man. Mabel and Laura had been told by their parents to stay away from the railway yard. But according to a story told by Willis both girls were crossing the tracks and passed by the private rail car in which he worked as a cook and porter.

He loved to tell the story of how he "accidentally" dropped a large pot on the ground causing a loud clatter as it hit the ground. Both girls looked up being somewhat startled. He climbed down from the train to retrieve the pot and then looked at the two girls and said "Did that frighten you? I am so terribly sorry." He then added ""Pardonez moi s'il vous plais." The latter phrase he had picked up in Montreal where he spent several years. But more later about how the Moores met.

Willis was the son of a former slave who had escaped from slavery and fled to Canada by way of the Underground Railroad. Willis' mother had escaped with his father. They married and Willis was one of three children. Willis' father became a spiritual leader to fellow escapees in Canada. Willis was born in New Brunswick and spent his early years there. At about age sixteen he moved to Montreal to experience the high life.

Charles and Louise moved into their new home when the baby (me) was about six months old. Little did they know that the baby would soon have an additional pair of parents.

Mr. McLane had several trucks which he used to move factory products from one place to another, usually from one factory to a warehouse or to a rail siding. He hired men from the neighborhood to load and unload the products. Charles occasionally worked for Mr. McLane, who was also from Virginia. When Charles and Louise got ready to move Charles asked Mr. McLane if he could use one of the trucks. Mr. McLane gave Charles permission and told Charles to ask one of the other men to help him with the move. Mr. McLane was a generous man who had created a carting company many years ago. He developed a reputation as a very careful but speedy cart driver. He soon acquired two additional carts and two more drivers. He went into the army in 1917. He became familiar with trucks while in the service and when he returned home in 1919 he purchased a truck and resumed his carting business. He soon owned several trucks and his business flourished. With all his success Mr. McLane never stopped working. He drove one of his trucks every day and helped load and unload. He was indeed a special man.

On the day of the move Charles went down to get the truck from the truck yard. When he arrived he saw Mr. McLane and Mr. McLane's nephew. Mr. McLane greeted Charles with a big smile and said, "Good morning Charlie, you just got lucky. I've got you a driver and a helper." Charles looked around and said, "Yes sir, who've I got?" Mr. McLane replied, "Me and Bobby, let's go!"

Charles tried not to show his shock and followed Mr. McLane to one of the big Mac trucks. Charles looked at the size of the truck and estimated that everything he and Louise owned wouldn't fill one quarter of that truck. He wanted to tell Mr. McLane this but he knew better than to question this gift. He climbed up into the cab of the truck next to Bobby.

When they arrived at Orchard Street Charles could not believe his eyes. All of his furniture was sitting on the sidewalk and three of Mr. McLane's men were sitting there with big grins on their faces.

The truck was expertly maneuvered to the curb and before Charles had time to say anything the three men began loading the truck. Mr. McLane told Charles to remain in the truck while it was being loaded. He also informed him that his wife and the baby were waiting for him over at the new house.

Mr. McLane told Charles that whenever one of his employees had to move he always provided a truck and help. Charles who was just a part-time employee could hardly believe his ears. He was told that when one of the other employees had need of help, Charles would be expected to offer his services.

When the loading was completed the loaders jumped on the back of the truck and Mr. McLane began the short drive to Gregory Street. Upon arrival at Gregory Street the truck again backed to the curb. Charles climbed down from the truck to help unload. But again, Mr. McLane told him to stand back and let the three men do the work. He also told him to go in the house and help his wife arrange furniture. Charles walked into the front hall and entered into the living room expecting to see Louise and the baby. They were not there. He walked into the dining room and then into the kitchen – still no Louise and baby. He walked into the bedroom just off the kitchen –nothing! He walked into the bathroom and through it to the front bedroom. There she was stretched out on a bed he had never before seen. He looked around the room and saw two other strange pieces of furniture, a dressing table and a large dresser. No words – just total surprise.

Mr. McLane called from the front door. "Charlie, where do you want this stuff to go?" Charles looked at Louise and she laughingly said "Surprised?" He nodded affirmatively. She said, "Me too."

Mr. McLane called again, "Charlie, where do you want this stuff?" Charles left the bedroom and went to assist the movers. Mr. McLane said "How'd you like the bedroom furniture?" Charles said, "Mr. McLane I don't know what to say." Mr. McLane said, "Thank you will be enough." "I don't know how I'll ever repay you," Charles said. "You don't owe me anything. I was moving some furniture from Chamberlains the other day and the people getting it didn't know what to do with their old stuff. I told them I thought I might have a place for it. It seems as though I found a place for it. One of the boys told me you were trying to find a bedroom set. Does your wife like it?" Charles replied, "Yes Sir!"

It dawned on Charles that Louise didn't have the baby with her in the bedroom. He went back into the house and started to call to Louise when he heard the baby's voice and loud laughter coming from upstairs. He asked Louise where the baby was. She said, "He's upstairs visiting our landlord."

Louise told Charles that Mrs. Moore had come downstairs to open the apartment for her and the movers. The baby immediately began to reach for Mrs. Moore's hair and succeeded in getting a handful.

Louise said, "I was so embarrassed." Mrs. Moore on the other hand reached over took the baby from her and started talking to the baby. The baby in turn began to talk back to Mrs. Moore. Charles said, "Talked? He can't talk yet." Louise said, "Oh, yes he can, at least Mrs. Moore and he were having a great conversation. She told him what a beautiful boy he was and he started smiling and saying something which Mrs. Moore seemed to understand. He then said something else and Mrs. Moore said he wants to go upstairs."

Charles looked quizzically at Louise and shook his head. He told Louise that other than yes, no and Da he could understand nothing the baby uttered. Louise said, "You should have been here. I swear he and Mrs. Moore were having a conversation." At that moment they heard loud laughter again coming from upstairs. Curiosity got to both of them and they went up the back stairs and peeked through the screen door leading to the kitchen. There, sitting on the kitchen table was the baby with a piece of toast in his hand gesticulating and evidently talking to Mrs. Moore. She appeared to be listening and when the baby paused would reply with words like "You're right." "Is that so?" Then the baby would hold forth again.

Louise and Charles couldn't believe what they saw and heard. Charles tapped on the door. Mrs. Moore turned in her chair and said, "Please come in." They entered and the baby began to laugh and uttered a loud "Da". The baby reached for Charles. Charles reached the baby and said "Do you want me to pick you up Boy?" To Charles' surprise the baby uttered a clear "Yes!"

Mrs. Moore told Charles and Louise what a wonderful morning she spent with "Sunny". She asked them what they called the baby. Charles spoke up and said, "We call him Baby Charles." She said she had been calling the baby "Sunny" because he had brightened her day so brilliantly.

Louise and Charles gathered up Sunny and went downstairs. The men that had been doing the moving were seated around the kitchen table and when Louise walked in they all stood. She smiled nicely and said "My! What fine gentlemen!" Sunny also commented but no one understood what he said. But Charles said "What Sunny said was who are you talking about Mama?" Everyone broke out in loud laughter, including Sunny.

The move was now completed and the Twymans were now residents of a fine new apartment. It was almost Christmas and Charles and Louise wanted this to be a special holiday. They talked about what they were going to buy the baby for Christmas; where the tree was going to be set up. They discussed whether or not they would invite family and friends over for Christmas dinner. Louise pointed out to Charles that her father was expecting the family to gather at his home for Christmas dinner.

Christmas dinner at Grandpa Allen's house was real special. First of all every child was expected to be there with their spouse. That meant Jake and Elizabeth, Katie and John, Major and Mercedes, Mary and Clarence, Jennie and Sol, William and of course Louise and Charles. Now there were a couple of new additions, Sunny and Solomon. Dorothy the daughter of Mary and Clarence had been there a couple of Christmas'. Sunny and Solomon were new and two years younger than Dorothy. Grandpa Allen believed in tradition and exhibited this each Christmas.

There were many things that happened to me and the family over the next few years. There were family conflicts and joyful incidents. I got to know my family, uncles, aunts, cousins and, to a somewhat lesser degree, my grandparents.

The stories of my uncles, if done properly could be developed into a movie. But as I stated earlier this would be a series of essays based upon my recollections.

As in all families fortunate enough to have uncles there are mother's brothers whom I call uncle and then there are dad's brothers whom I also call uncle. However we cannot forget dad's sisters' husbands and mom's sisters' husbands whom I also call uncle. There are varying shades, flavors, shapes and sizes of uncles. Some are most exciting, some are interesting and some we never really get to know. Those I got to know were truly distinctive.

Now I've referred to my Uncle John who was my mother's brother-in-law. I like to refer to Uncle John as my rich uncle. Every family should have a rich uncle.

Sunday, Sunday

Sunday has always been a special day in my life. Sunday was the day when there was a special breakfast served at our table. It was the day that Dad got up real early and began preparation for making spoon bread. He also changed the water in which the salt mackerel were being freshened.

Mother, that's what I called her at that time, was usually busy in the bathroom getting ready for church. She never got fully dressed because she said Daddy's salt mackerel smelled up her church clothes. So she usually came to the table with her bathrobe on.

Daddy broke the eggs, separated them, beat the whites and the yolks. He then stirred the cornmeal mush which he had put on the stove a few minutes earlier. Mother came into the kitchen and started to fill the percolator with water and coffee. Dad beat the egg whites again and began to mix all of the ingredients so that he had a large bowl of spoon bread batter.

I remember one particular Sunday Mother said "Sunny did you study your Bible verse for Sunday School?" I replied "Yes, Mother." She then told me to take out knives, forks, and spoons and to set the table. This was a job that my cousin Amelia used to do.

"Well," Dad said, "I'm about ready to fry the fish. Everybody sit down." Now I don't know if you have ever smelled fresh coffee percolating, fish frying and spoon bread in the oven. Please take it from me it is an indescribably delicious combination of smells. If you weren't hungry I guarantee you would become ravenously hungry. Dad would remove the fried fish from the iron skillet and place them on a plate. Mother would place the platter on the table. She would then pour coffee in her cup and in Daddy's cup. On Sunday morning she would pour about one teaspoon of coffee in my cup and then fill it with hot cocoa which she had made.

Now came the great moment when Daddy would open the oven door, and bring out the beautiful baking dish of spoon bread. For the uninitiated – spoon bread is a soufflé'. It is a light, custard bread with a crusty top and a melt in your mouth body. Daddy was an expert at making the wonderful dish and we looked forward to it on Sunday mornings.

We usually said grace before the bread was brought to the table. The reason for this was simple. We all wanted to see this wonderful concoction arrive at the table with its beautiful golden brown top hat.

Dad would set the dish carefully down on the table so that the soufflé' would not fall. He then took a large serving spoon, plunged into the middle of the wonderful dish and it deflated allowing a wonderful buttery aroma to fill the air. He then served each plate with a large portion of the lovely, light, fluffy spoon bread. Mother placed a piece of butter on the bread. I loved to watch the rich golden streams of melted butter run down the bread and make a little golden pool at the base of the round golden delight.

Later that morning we went to church. I always got there in time for Sunday School. Yes, I got there with memories of spoon bread, fried salt mackerel and my special coffee.

Sunday School

Thinking back to my Sunday School days my mind immediately turned to a particular Sunday.

I was a garrulous nine year old and had been placed in the 9-12 boys' class by Mrs. Bunn, Superintendent of the Sunday School at the Bethel AME Church. We met in the church basement in small cubicles called classrooms. Mrs. Bunn's desk set on a low platform in front of the room. There was a small bell on the desk and a Bible.

Each class had a person designated as leader. Our leader was a young man named James. James was rather small in stature. He also sang tenor in the choir.

The boys in our class loved to tease James about his stature and his rather high pitched voice. He would tell Mrs. Bunn. This threat was very effective since Mrs. Bunn had carte blanche from our parents to discipline us to whatever degree she deemed necessary. Our group probably had more visits from Mrs. Bunn than any of the other classes. I had no experience in this realm. However, James reminded me every Sunday that he would report any infraction that I committed.

Well on this particular Sunday I got to Sunday school earlier than usual because Mother and Daddy had to be at church early. They both sang in the choir and the choir director wanted a brief rehearsal before service. Mother had asked if I was ready for Sunday school. This meant had I completed any assignments given to my class.

We could hear the choir rehearsing and the piano thumping. The buzz of voices from the other classes was in the air. James got our attention and then asked how many of us had completed our assignment. Each one raised his hand.

James then asked Andrew the biggest boy in the class to recite his bible verse (This by the way was our assignment). Andrew gave his bible verse which was rather lengthy. I remember thinking that this was great. If everyone's verse was that long maybe by the time James got to me class would be over.

No such luck, though several of the other boys had long passages it soon came to me.

You may recall that I had told my mother that I had prepared myself for Sunday school. Well this was the usual pattern on Sunday morning. We sat the table having Sunday breakfast and just before getting up from the table Mother would ask "Are you ready for Sunday school? I don't want to hear that you didn't do your lessons." My answer was always the same, "Yes Mother." This was always true – well, to a degree.

Getting back to this particular Sunday I had most certainly prepared myself. I had perused the Bible diligently seeking a verse that I could recite. I listened with admiration as my classmates recited their verses.

Now it was my turn. My diligence provided me with the following, "Jesus wept."

And so did I when Mother heard from Mrs. Bunn and James.

Starlight-Star Bright

One thing that is patently clear especially in recent days is – If a thought comes into your head and you want to retain it – write it down.

As I was writing about going off to the army and my dad embracing me and kissing me on the cheek, this brought to mind an incident that happened when I was about three years old.

When I was a little guy and my parents wanted to go out to an evening affair they took me along. I remember going with my parents to visit family and friends. Usually there were other folks there with their children. We were usually put in the room where the coats and hats were placed. Needless to say this was heaven for kids two, three and four years old. I remember trying on hats and coats and making believe that I was an adult. We really had fun.

Usually we got home in the dark of night and I was usually asleep by the time we got there. I recall waking up in the morning and wondering how I got in my bed.

On a particular evening my folks were at a friend's house and I remember my dad coming into the room to get his and mother's coats. This time I was wide awake which I think surprised my dad.

He took me by the hand and walked out with me and mother's coat. Good-byes were said and we started home. I walked between my parents. Then Dad picked me up and placed me on his shoulders. This was a special treat especially since it was dark outside.

I remember turning my head to look at my mother. Suddenly a huge yellow ball appeared in the sky. I remember gripping my dad tightly around the neck and screaming out, "Daddy, Daddy, there's a big light in the sky!"

My dad stopped and pointed to the large light in the sky and said, "That's the moon." Mother then said, "Look at all the little lights up there. They are stars." She then sang a song that had these words – "Star light, Star bright, First star I've seen tonight." Then Dad put me down on the sidewalk, gave me a kiss on the cheek and said, "You are growing up little man."

Fried Pies and Chowder

Food has always played an important part in my family's life. From a very early stage in my life I can recall numerous discussions about the preparations of various foods ranging from game to pancakes. I remember how we joyfully anticipated Grandma Twyman's arrival from Virginia. Her arrival was always preceded by the arrival of a large barrel of goodies from the farm.

The barrel usually arrived about a week before Grandma. It was a large container called a hogshead. I remember my dad saying that his uncle made the barrels. What was in the barrel was of greater interest to me.

When the barrel arrived the man driving the Railway Express truck rang our door bell and asked where we wanted the barrel placed. He and his helper would then unload the large barrel onto a hand truck and roll it around to the back of the house. Mother, my dad, Cousin Amelia and I gathered around the barrel and Dad took the top hoop from around the barrel and removed the burlap covering. Under the covering there was a white cloth, sort of like a large white sheet. Then he reached down and brought up a large bundle and handed it to my mother. She opened it and the smell of apples filled the air. Inside the cloth wrapped package was an abundance of cream colored dried apples. Following the package of apples came a package of dried peaches and then a burlap bag of raw peanuts, sweet potatoes, corn meal and lard and finally a slab of bacon and a ham. All of these delicious treats were neatly packed and I was ready to have a feast. My mother gave me and Amelia a chance to help ourselves to the dried apples and peaches.

Upon my grandmother's arrival we looked forward to the good food that she would cook. One thing I still drool over is the memory of her fried apple pies. Those pies were doubtless the best apple pies ever. She also made peach pies that were probably as good but apple was my favorite.

I watched her prepare the pies and remember her rinsing the dried apples and then putting them in a pot with a little water, sugar and spices and a pinch of salt. She made a pie crust using the lard which she had sent. Once the dried apples had stewed and cooled she cut circles of pie crust, filled and folded them over. She then put the pies into a large iron kettle half full of hot lard. When the pies were nice and brown she took them out and put them on a large piece of brown paper, usually a paper bag that had been torn open. After several minutes she would sprinkle them with powdered sugar. Then she would give me one.

My mother began to make these delicious fried pies and my dad would take them to his job and sell them for five cents.

There were other cooks in the family who made dishes that have left a lasting impression on me. One of those persons was my Uncle John.

Uncle John was a professional cook. He hardly ever cooked at home. Home cooking was Aunt Katie's domain. But, I had a chance to see and experience Uncle John's cooking. I worked part-time as a kitchen helper at the Yale secret society where he was employed. The food that he prepared at Yale is best described as plain food. He did not believe in what he called fancy food. He believed in the liberal use of cream and butter.

The 22nd of February was a big day at Uncle John's place. The menu consisted of chicken a la king, roast prime rib of beef, green peas and mashed potatoes. Dessert was ice cream and sliced strawberries.

This dinner was not the object of my attention. It was the stock in which the chickens were cooked. Most of the time it was turkeys rather than chickens. He saved the stock cooled and froze it. About five months later when the college was closed we went to the kitchen and retrieved the frozen stock.

He usually had a dozen large cohog clams and about a bushel of cherrystone clams. Sometime he had razor clams (they are delicious.) He washed the cohogs and put them into a large stock pot which he let boil until the cohogs opened. He then removed the clams, discarded the shells, chopped up the meat. Uncle John would then add the thawed turkey stock.

My job was to peel the potatoes, take onions and celery and cut them into small pieces. Sometimes if we had carrots I would peel and cut them up. Once my peeling and cutting was done Uncle John had me open a case of canned tomatoes and about three large cans of tomato sauce. While I was doing this Uncle John diced up about a pound and a half of salt pork which he rinsed off and then fried up. He added the chopped up onions and celery. After awhile he added this to the clam/turkey stock. He cooked this for a while and then added the tomatoes and tomato sauce and the potatoes and carrots. The last thing he added was the chopped up clam meat, black pepper and sugar.

When this concoction was finally cooked about an hour or so he and I would lift the pots from the stove and immerse them in cold water until they got cold. The next day we took it to the camp grounds where our club outing was to be held.

Some of the club members would have built a large fire in a stone lined pit upon which sat a huge cast iron kettle. We, upon our arrival, took the large pots of soup and poured them into the iron kettle filling it to the top. Uncle John then added his secret ingredient – two one pound blocks of butter.

The soup was ready when the butter melted and was stirred into the soup. It was amazing to see how fast that soup disappeared.

When I began writing this piece I had no intention of dwelling on Uncle John's clam soup. However, once I started I could literally taste it. It was so rich and delicious.

Uncle John refused to call it Manhattan clam chowder. He said that clam chowder had to have milk and cream in it. He called his recipe clam soup. Whatever it was I just called it good and like Grandma Twyman's fried apple pies it left a lasting impression on me and my appreciation of good food all these many years of my life.

Young people today need the experience of seeing, smelling and tasting good food prepared with love, care, and pride. It does make a difference.

Christmas Eve

I'm not sure how I got to this point in my writing. But my mind began dwelling on Shirley, Norman and William. These three had a great influence on my life. Their mother, Ethel and my mother were friends and we lived in the same neighborhood. My cousin Amelia and Shirley were about the same age and were six years older than me and Will. Norman (Slim) was two years older than Will.

Will, Norm and I used to play together. They were special friends. I think it was because they lived with their mother (whom I called Aunt Ethel) and their grandmother, Mrs. Sturgis and their great-grandparents Mr. and Mrs. Wiley.

Mr. Wiley was the owner of a horse and wagon and needless to say this in itself made Norm and Will special. Their great-grandfather used to let them ride in the wagon and if I happened to be with them I too would be allowed to ride. We also had the "pleasure" of cleaning the stall. I say pleasure because Mr. Wiley told us this was so. But Norm, Will and I learned that horse manure had monetary value. We began to sell small bags of manure to some of the neighborhood gardeners. Prior to our discovery of the monetary value of manure, people used to just come over to the barn and help themselves. No more free manure once Will, Norm and I found that a small bag of manure was worth a dime. You might think that Mr. Wiley's horse's output had to be prodigious. No, there were two other horses in the barn and we cleaned their stalls as well. The money we earned came in handy for special occasions.

Christmas Eve was a special time for Norm, Will, Shirley, Amelia and me. This was the day that we did our Christmas shopping. Amelia and Shirley being the oldest took Will, Norm and me downtown to visit the big stores. We went into Malley's, Gamble and Desmond, Shartenbergs and Stanley's. We also visited the 5 and 10 Cent stores, Kresge's, Woolworths and Grants. The latter three are where we did our shopping for gifts. Though we, by this time, didn't strongly believe that Santa was real, we still visited the Santa's in all three department stores. We watched from a distance as little children went to talk with the jolly man with the big belly. We didn't notice at that time – but thinking back- all of the children talking to Santa were white.

After our shopping tour our next stop was at a large delicatessen on State Street. Amelia and Shirley who had responsibility for the money, purchased large containers of cole slaw, potato salad and until this day I believe the best frankfurts ever. They then marched us uptown to Shirley, Will and Norman's house or to my and Amelia's house. Whoever's house we knew there would be baked beans in the oven, cocoa on the stove and brownies waiting.

This was indeed our day. Amelia and I usually wrapped our presents to Mother in special paper that Amelia bought. Norm, Shirley and Will did likewise. We then exchanged little token gifts to each other. Then we would sit down (i.e. Will, me and Norman) and wait while Shirley and Amelia fixed our plates with the delicious frankfurts, potato salad, cole slaw and baked beans. If we were at Norm and Will, and Shirley's the baked beans were sweet light brown. At our house the beans were sweet and dark brown. My mother's baked beans had molasses and Will's mom used brown sugar and syrup. However both were delicious and were loaded with salt pork which usually got crispy on top.

After our feast we would wish each other "Merry Christmas" and go home.

As I stated at the beginning of this piece, I'm not sure how I got to this point. It was a sweet, tasty journey. Thanks for coming along.

Fear

Very few people that I've been acquainted with over the years have ever voluntarily admitted to being fearful. Most people, especially men, avoid any reference to fear unless urged by someone else. Well I haven't been urged by anyone but it would only be fair to anyone reading my stories to know that I am one of those persons who never wished to admit to being fearful. But, I am. I think most of my life I've been afraid of something.

Looking back to my very early years I recall a particular incident that tested my ability to overcome fear.

One morning during the summer of my ninth year I was outside playing with some of my friends. You need to have a picture in your mind of the setting in which this test took place. Mr. Hoffman owned three pieces of property near the corner of Dixwell Avenue and Gregory Street. In the rear of the property was the foundation of an unfinished building. It was quite deep, probably 12 – 14 feet. There was a wooden platform that extended out about six feet all around the foundation. On the platform there was a track that supported a crane. Mr. Hoffman used the crane to lower and raise scrap metal which he collected. The crane was operated by a series of ropes and pulleys. The kids in the neighborhood were prohibited from playing in this area. Such a prohibition was, of course, an invitation to play.

So on this particular summer morning my buddies and I went to play around the "hole." This is what we called the unfinished foundation. The older boys had rigged a long piece of towing rope to the top of Mr. Hoffman's crane. The rope was used to swing from one side of the "hole" to the other during a game of <u>Follow the Leader</u>.

My friend Junie was the leader on this particular day. He had athletic skills that were way beyond my capabilities; however I tried to emulate his moves. Though I was the youngest in the group, I was not the smallest. I was rather tall, but I was quite thin.

Junie ran, climbed and jumped over and around every obstacle on the property. I was able to do most of the feats that the leader did, maybe a little less artful, but nevertheless I was able to keep up.

We had been playing about twenty minutes when Junie held up his hand and announced that anyone who failed the next text would get a "noogie." Now everyone dreaded getting a "noogie." A "noogie" in a group meant getting a punch on your bicep by everyone in the group. "Noogies" hurt, especially if you were skinny like me.

The final test was to swing across the "hole" on the rope attached to Mr. Hoffman's crane, let go and land safely on the other side of the hole. One might think this is a rather easy task; and it is if you don't have a fear of height.

The distance across the "hole" as I recall, was about sixty feet. When you're nine, sixty feet looks to be as wide as the Atlantic Ocean. If one factors in the depth of the hole then the "hole" becomes a chasm.

I can still sense the fear that came over me with the announcement that we would either follow the leader or get a "noogie." I realized at that moment that I was "scairt" really, really "scairt." I knew I could deal with the pain of the "noogie," but I didn't know how to deal with the possibility of failure, especially in front of my friends. I had seen and heard how "scaredy cats" were dealt with by my friends (and I). It would be tough enough to be called "scaredy cat" and worse "coward". But the ultimate ignominy would be isolation from the group.

One by one the guys swung across the "hole". It was finally Herbie's turn. He was just ahead of me. Herbie was skinny like me. In fact, he was even skinnier. He grabbed the rope and backed away from the edge of the "hole". He stopped for a minute or two and then ran toward the "hole and jumped out into space. I watched him swing toward the opposite side then let go. He seemed to be suspended in air and then he landed. The other successful flyers all cheered when Herbie landed.

It was now my turn. The rope hung limply from Mr. Hoffman's crane. I eyed it and then looked down to the bottom of the "hole". I couldn't keep my eyes from staring across the wide opening, which defined, the "hole". The "hole" was taking on a whole new dimension in my mind.

The "hole" became a chasm, a wide evil place just waiting to swallow me up. I started to shake and to breathe in gulps of air. I could hear the shouts from my friends. "C'mon Sunny! C'mon Sunny!!" I walked to where the limp rope hung. I reached for it and couldn't grasp it. I tried again and couldn't reach the rope. Then I heard Junie's voice, "Hey Sunny, stretch your arms." Somehow Junie saw through my ploy to claim that I couldn't reach the rope. It was true that I really hadn't extended my arms out to capture the rope. I really did not want to – I was scared to death.

Finally I got a grip on the rope. I discovered that there was a huge knot at the end of the rope. I gripped the rope much as a drowning person might grasp a life saving ring. If the rope had been a living entity I would most certainly have killed it. I took another look down at what was now a yawning crevasse – an awesome chasm.

No way was I going to swing over this sea of blood thirsty sharks – this den of man eating lions – this fiery furnace. My name was not Jonah, nor was it Daniel, nor Meschach, nor Abednego. I was Sunny and I was scared.

Then all the guys on the other side began to scream, "Come on Sunny the Hun is coming." That was our name for Mr. Hoffman. I turned to see if they were telling the truth. They were indeed. They now were imploring me to swing across. Mr. Hoffman came toward me. He was holding a shovel in his hand and he seemed to be focusing on me.

Without hesitation any longer I ran toward the "hole" and jumped. I didn't leap as my buddies had – I jumped holding onto the rope. I went down and came to an abrupt stop dangling from the end of the rope. The rope didn't move. The guys kept yelling, "Kick Sunny! Kick!! Make the rope move." I tried to no avail. I held on, afraid to let go.

All of a sudden I felt the rope tighten and I was suddenly above the rim of the "hole" and then found myself moving toward the opposite side of the "hole". I felt hands on my dangling feet and legs. I was too frightened to look down. I heard Junie's voice saying, "Let go the rope Sunny. Let go." I let go. When I touched the ground I opened my eyes and gazed across the chasm and saw Mr. Hoffman winding the handle on the crane. I saw the rope which I had clung to moving toward the other side.

My buddies were all laughing and patting me on the back. Junie told them that since I had made it to the other side there would be no "noogies."

That experience served me well many years later when I was a sergeant in the Army of the U.S. Thanks to Mr. Hoffman.

Jam Kee

One of my boyhood dreams was to see various places in the world. Of course the world of my youth was a much smaller place than it is now.

The world of my youth encompassed the forty-eight states, Canada, Mexico, some islands of the Caribbean , most of Europe and a limited knowledge of the biblical middle east. I knew little about the Pacific Ocean islands. China and India were also a part of my world.

So my boyhood dream of seeing the world focused upon Europe and China. Europe held an interest for me because this was the focus of my school geographical studies. China became interesting to me because of Jam Kee.

You probably wonder what is Jam Kee? A better question would be, "Who is Jam Kee?"

Jam Kee was the owner of a hand laundry in my neighborhood. He was a very quiet, almost reclusive person who had little to say other than respond to questions such as, "When will my laundry be ready?" or "How much is this going to cost?"

My first recollection of Jam Kee was when my mother sent me to the Chinese laundry with some of my father's shirts. She had not been feeling well and was not able to do the laundry. She sent the sheets, towels and other things to the big laundry but Dad's shirts had to be hand laundered.

As I entered Jam Kee's laundry the smell of clean, freshly washed and ironed laundry permeated the air. I can only describe the smell as clean. There was no smell of chemicals.

There was no perfumed soap smell. It was just a smell of clean.

The air in the small space that contained Jam Kee's laundry was small. It consisted of a counter that extended from one side of the small space to the other. It was about three feet wide. At that time in my life I could just see over the counter. I was nine years old.

This was the first time I had ever seen Jam Kee up close. In fact it was the first time I'd ever seen a Chinaman. The color was different than I had ever seen before. He was sort of yellow, but not really yellow; maybe more tan with a yellow pink tint. His eyes were different in that they seemed to be almost closed. But I could tell that, unlike my Mom or Dad's eyes or my cousin Amelia's, his eyes were black. His hair was black and slick.

My observation was cut short by a voice that was different from anything I had heard before. "What you want boy?" The voice was sort of high pitched, yet not unpleasant. I was startled because I had been staring at Jam Kee somewhat wide eyed. I was doing what my mother had cautioned me to never do. That is, not to stare or gape at anyone different than myself. I indeed did both. I stared and gaped.

I finally told the Chinese laundry man that my mother had sent me to have my father's shirts washed and ironed.

The laundryman wanted to know if my mother said to starch the shirts. I told him that my mother wanted starch. He then said, "You come three day."

Upon returning home I asked my mother if Jam Kee was white or colored. She thought about it for a few seconds and laughed. Then she said, "He's Chinese." So at that point in my life I learned that there were now three groups of people in the world that I lived in – White, Colored and Chinese.

Friends and Dads

In my world, which at that time was a little over nine years old, white people made up a vast majority. My best friends, Raymond, Johnny and Joe, were important to me. I had known Raymond since I was two years old. Johnny and Joe came into my life when I was seven. Raymond was of German-Polish background. Johnny was Italian and Joe was Jewish.

Raymond's father was a veteran of World War I and was a motorman on a trolley car. Johnny's father was a shoemaker and Joe's father owned a news and candy store.

I mention my friends' fathers because they all treated me well.

Ray's father as previously stated was a veteran of World War I. He was a member of the American Legion and was also a member of the group known as the 40 and 8. The 40 and 8 took its name from the French rail cars that could carry 40 men and 8 horses. He was a real nice man and was active in politics. But his outstanding quality to me was the fact that he operated a trolley car.

Ray's mom used to make sandwiches for her husband to take to work. Sometimes on Saturdays she would make soup or another hot dish. On these days Ray would take the hot dish to the corner of Dixwell and Gregory and his Dad would stop the trolley car. Ray would jump aboard and off they would go. On a few occasions I would go with Ray and be invited to ride to the end of the line.

At the end of the line Ray (and I, once or twice) would prepare the trolley for the return trip downtown. During this interim period Ray's dad would eat his lunch. The most important thing however was that Ray's dad let him move the trolley a few feet by handling the control lever. He let me try it once. What a thrill!!

Now Joe's dad was different. He was a quiet man who always greeted me with a pat on the head and a nod toward the rear of the store where the family lived. It was here that Joe's mom made the very best chicken soup that I have ever tasted. What I remember most was the little pullet eggs that were cooked with the soup and there was always a bowl for me.

Johnny's father was the owner, operator of Patsy's, a shoe repair shop. Patsy was the most dynamic of all my friend's dads. He was the father of six, three boys and three girls. He lived with his family in a house to which his business was attached.

Historically the period about which I write was 1930-1931. It was the height of the Great Depression. My dad had lost a very good job as a chauffeur for a very rich publisher in New Jersey. My mother was pregnant and things were tough.

I have to be careful as to how I describe this period in my life. It is so easy to define that period in today's vernacular. So when I say things were tough, I mean that we had very little money. Mother was pregnant. Dad had a job as a houseman/butler at Yale. He and my mother had shared the job until she became pregnant. They worked for a well known research physician. So by the standards of that period in history we were doing pretty well. We ate regularly and we had a roof over our heads.

I guess we were doing quite well. Just the year before when my father lost his job the bank in which our savings were deposited closed. Now that was a tough time. By the grace of God and the unwillingness of my parents to give up – we survived. Of course we had help. My grandparents in Virginia sent us food. My grandfather in New Haven gave us eggs and chickens and my Uncle John and Aunt Catherine used to send us butter and milk which found its way to our house from the kitchen where my uncle worked.

We had food and to all outward appearances we were doing well.

But getting back to my expanding world and my friends Raymond, Johnny and Joe, none of us had any spending money unless we earned it. Raymond and I sold magazines and did errands for people in the neighborhood.

We received no money for selling magazines. We sold Saturday Evening Post and Liberty magazines and received coupons which we could redeem for prizes. I wanted a bicycle more than anything in the world. But one had to sell hundreds of magazines to accumulate enough coupons to redeem them for a bicycle.

The system was designed to keep the boy's noses to the grindstone. You earned two green coupons for every five magazines you sold. For every ten green coupons you could exchange them for one brown coupon. Ten browns could be exchanged for one gold coupon. The coupons were called greenies, brownies, and goldies. A bicycle could be gotten for 500 goldies.

Neither Ray nor I ever acquired a bicycle. But I accumulated a cigar box full of greenies, brownies and a few goldies. Our boss, the man who supplied us with magazines disappeared and with him our hopes for a bicycle.

My need for cash increased when my interests in dill pickles from Mr. Hadelman's delicatessen was awakened. I also discovered a new necessity - Doughnuts. My interests in pickles and doughnuts came about when one of my classmates brought a large dill pickle to class wrapped in a small brown paper bag. The smell of garlic and dill was enough to drive me crazy. I had tasted dill pickles at Joe's house but only a slice at a time. But the pickle in the brown bag was huge and the smell indescribably delicious. I just had to have a pickle of my own.

I overheard some boys talking about the Elm City Cruller Bakery just a few blocks from where I lived. What I heard was that if you went to the Elm City Cruller Bakery early in the morning the bakers would sell you a bag of broken crullers for ten cents.

Again one of my classmates had a bag of broken crullers which his brother had given him. He shared his largess with me and several of his friends on the schoolyard one morning. The broken pieces were crispy, sweet and absolutely delicious. I really needed to get some money so that I could buy a bag of broken crullers.

So you can now understand my need for cash. I had to have pickles and doughnuts.

722nd Medical Sanitary Company
Philippines, October 1945

My dad, Charles L. Twyman, Circa, 1941
New Haven, Connecticut

Seated in the center
Recruited escort at Girl Friends' Conclave
Taft Hotel, New Haven
Circa 1941

As Senior Warden with Clarence Coolridge,
Bishop of Connecticut, at St. Luke's Episcopal Church,
New Haven, March 23, 1986

First day on job as New Haven's first appointed
African-American school principal, 1963

With Richard Timpson (back row, second right) and
and other fellow warriors of The Ashanti Club
Circa 1968

In New Guinea, 1945

U.S. Army, 1943

*With welterweight champion Sugar Ray Robinson, and
Heavyweight champion Sgt. Joe Louis, Camp Edwards,
Falmouth, Massachusetts, August 30, 1943*

My sister, Alyce

My mother, Louise Twyman (Second row, first left)
with Dramu (Drama, Art, Music Club) 1938

Mother (Second row, second right) with cast from
"Duberry Brown", 1939 World's Fair

My mother
Teacher of children with special needs
Bridgeport, Connecticut

THE CITY OF NEW HAVEN

and

THE DIXWELL NEIGHBORHOOD RENEWAL COMMITTEE
In recognition of the faith in their neighborhood which property owners in the Dixwell Area are showing, extend their congratulations to   *JOHN ROBINSON*
for completing the rehabilitation of the property   located at   *308 DIXWELL AVE.*   in the Dixwell Renewal Area and are pleased to present this

CERTIFICATE OF ACHIEVEMENT

HONORABLE RICHARD C. LEE
MAYOR, CITY OF NEW HAVEN

CHARLES TWYMAN, CHAIRMAN
DIXWELL NEIGHBORHOOD RENEWAL COMMITTEE

Certificate presented from proud nephew to uncle

Jam Kee – Once More

This takes me back to Jam Kee. You will recall that Jam Kee told me to come back in three days to pick up my father's shirts. Well I went to the laundry to get my dad's shirts and did so without incident. The shirts were neatly folded and laid on sheets of brown wrapping paper. I paid him with the money that had been given me. Jam Kee admonished, "You no drop laundry!" I got the shirts home with no problem.

Later that afternoon while playing with my wagon I passed in front of Jam Kee's laundry. I heard a voice call out, "Hey boy! You!" I looked about and saw Jam Kee. He was standing at the door to his store and beckoned to me to come to him. My first inclination was to run by with my wagon.

Jam Kee waited as I hesitantly pulled the wagon over to the laundry door. He stood there waiting until I stopped. He handed me a piece of paper with the name of the family that lived next door to me.

Jam Kee said "You take laundry," and pointed to my wagon. I didn't know what to say so I nodded affirmatively. He went into the laundry and retuned with two packages of laundry. It looked like sheets and towels. He put the packages down into my wagon and said, "You take!" He then gave me a nickel.

I took the laundry to the address on the piece of paper knocked on the door and delivered the laundry. The lady to whom I delivered the laundry told me to wait and when she returned she handed me a nickel. This was an unexpected windfall. I had earned my first ten cents. This revelation that work produced cash served me well during the next few years of my youth.

I couldn't wait to tell Johnny and to inform him of my plan to go down to the Elm City Cruller Company to purchase a bag of broken crullers. I didn't find Johnny and so I placed my knee onto the bed of the wagon, grasped the handle and pushed off with my left foot. I sped down Dixwell Avenue at top foot speed. I covered the seven and a half blocks in about ten minutes. The sidewalk traffic was relatively light which meant that I did not run anyone down.

I arrived at the cruller bakery and tried the door; it was locked. Not to panic!! I grasped the handle of my wagon and walked down the alley to the rear of the bakery. There was no sign of anyone either inside or outside. My spirits began to fall. Then I recalled my friend saying his brother went to the bakery early in the morning.

I made my way slowly up Dixwell Avenue. Anyone who saw me during my return trip would have thought I'd just lost my best friend.

About midway up the Avenue I looked across and wonder of wonders I saw Mr. Hadelman's delicatessen the source of the best dill pickles in the whole world.

There was not a moment's hesitation. I darted across the Avenue and into the delicatessen. Out of breath I literally shouted, "One pickle please." Mr. Hadelman's wife reached into the pickle barrel, fished about and came up with the biggest pickle that I'd ever seen. She put it in a small brown paper bag and handed it to me. I reached into my pocket and handed her one of my two nickels. I had just spent my own money. Money I earned on something which I coveted.

I made my way back across Dixwell Avenue to retrieve my wagon. But there was no wagon. It had disappeared. I searched and inquired but no one had seen my wagon. No wagon!!

I've been all over the place with this story. My desire to see the world would have to be delayed for awhile due to the loss of my wagon.

I walked slowly up the Avenue holding tightly to my dill pickle with tears in my eyes. As I walked by Jam Kee's laundry I heard his voice call "Boy. You boy." I went into the laundry and Jam Kee said, "You take laundry to Mrs. Rasmussen." I told Jam Kee that I'd lost my wagon. He nodded then said you take laundry in my new wagon," pointing to a wagon loaded with laundry. My wagon!!!

Jam Kee did something I didn't think he could do. He smiled!

I made the delivery and earned another nickel. My wagon and I went home. I had no crullers but I had ten cents and half a dill pickle in a soggy brown paper bag.

Books

Several days ago my wife and I were talking about establishing a collection of books and I told her about a friend of my parents who was an idol of mine. His name was James Whyte.

James Whyte was a World War I veteran and a man who loved books. As was the custom at that time (1920's) I called Mr. Whyte, Uncle Jim because he was a frequent visitor in our home. Uncle Jim and my father often played tennis together.

Uncle Jim had a private library. It was actually a room in his rental apartment which he shared with his son James Whyte III. Every wall of the room which housed Uncle Jim's books was covered with shelf after shelf of books. What has stayed with me all these years is that each book had glued to its inside front cover a book shield with Uncle Jim's personal monogram. Young Jim and I spent a great deal of time in the library perusing books that were far beyond the comprehension of a couple of eight year olds.

One day while Uncle Jim was at work, he was a postal clerk, Jim and I decided to be nosey. We looked in drawers, closets, in cabinets and cupboards. As I recall we didn't find anything of interest. There was one place that was off limits to Jim – that was his dad's bedroom.

This particular summer day was an exceedingly boring one so we entered into the sanctum sanctorum – Uncle Jim's bedroom. This breach was an act of extraordinary bravery on Jim's part. He had been told by his dad that such an intrusion would result in very serious consequences.

One must keep in mind the power of boredom and the lengths to which two eight year old boys will go to off set the effects of a boring afternoon. Three days before the foray into Uncle Jim's bedroom we had climbed the mulberry tree in Jim's backyard. We climbed as high as possible, got comfortable and started throwing very ripe berries at the windows of the house next door. We also ate as many berries as we could. Ripe mulberries are very sweet and too many can have a devastating effect on the stomach. We both had a serious case of diarrhea.

Getting back to the fateful afternoon when we entered Uncle Jim's bedroom. Jim warned me not to touch anything. As we entered I noticed that there were more shelves all filled with books. All of these book were leather bound and had gold lettering. We looked around and other than books there was nothing of interest. Something told me to look under the bed. I took a quick glance.

That was a fateful glance. There was a large jar sitting there. I reached under and pulled the jar out. It was almost filled with cherries and some kind of liquid. Jim gasped and in a loud whisper said, "Sunny put that back!!" I started to put it back but stopped when I got a whiff of something that was very intriguing.

I unscrewed the top and the perfume of liquor permeated the room. Without a word I reached into the jar and pulled out a cherry. Never had I tasted anything like this. It was sweet, slightly bitter and just a little sour. My mouth burned but not in a bad way. I told Jim to try one. He tried one and then another and I tried another and another. Together we must have eaten about one fourth of the jar.

Jim said he felt funny and I also noted that I felt funny like I was dizzy. I pushed the jar back under the bed and Jim and I left the room and went downstairs to sit on the back stoop. It was a hot afternoon. Jim and I fell asleep. When I awakened I tried to stand up and fell down to the ground. Jim awoke and started to stand and he too fell. We both began to laugh.

I told Jim I had to go home and proceeded to go in that direction. My house was about two and a half blocks away. My first few steps were unbelievably difficult. I felt as though I was walking up a steep hill and for some reason everything around me seemed to be moving in circles. It was sort of like when you spun around real fast and then tried to walk.

How long or in fact how I got home I can't tell you. I do remember my cousin saying that I smelled awful. In fact she said, "You stink."

I woke up in my bed and was surprised to see that it was dark outside. My mother peeked in the room and said rather sternly – "Get up and come out here." My head felt funny but the world wasn't spinning. When I walked out of my room and into the kitchen I was shocked to see Uncle Jim.

It was evident that he had told my mother what I had done that afternoon. Though she didn't say anything I knew I was going to be punished. I learned later that Jim had been punished for what we had done. I received a beating later that night.

Part of my punishment was that I was not allowed to leave the house for one week. I also had to write Uncle Jim a letter to apologize for what I had done. But a good thing happened. I had to spend the afternoon reading.

I began my library that week. I read four "big" little books which I stored in my room. I've never come close to Uncle Jim's collection and I never commissioned any book plates, but I learned to love reading and collecting books.

Uncle Jim died many years ago and his book collection was turned over to the New Haven African American Historical Society.

April 19, 2007

Seventy-six years ago, on or about the twentieth of April, my sister Alyce came home from the hospital with my mother. This was Alyce's first venture to the world outside the hospital.

Though I had never met my sister I had heard a lot about her from my dad and my aunts. I had also been given the honor by my parents of naming my sister. My dad had been to the hospital to visit one day and when he came home he told me that he and Mother had decided that I would be the one to name my sister.

Neither Mother nor Dad said a word about what a pain in the butt I had been. I had really touched every nerve that Dad had because I was not allowed to visit the hospital to visit Mother and to see my new sister. The last time I had seen Mother was on the fifth of April when I saw her lying on the floor of the basement at Bethel AME Church. I didn't know at that time that she had fainted on her way downstairs. I do remember seeing her leave the choir loft and come down the aisle. I do remember her smiling at me as she passed by. I do remember hearing a woman's scream and seeing people rush by me to the vestibule. I remember seeing the look on Dad's face as he rushed by and I remember running after him and yelling, "What's the matter Daddy?" It was then that I looked down the stairs and saw Mother.

In retrospect and with the addition of several courses in child development and psychology I now understand why I was a royal pain in my dad's butt. No one had explained to me what had happened to Mother.

April 20, 1931 was the day that my sister came home. This was the day that Mother was coming home. Indeed this day signified for me my stature as a very special member of the Twyman family. I not only attained the status of "Big Brother," I also was given the honor of naming my baby sister.

Alice Helen Louise arrived home amid much fanfare. My godmother Helen Daly, my mother's godmother Alice Chambers and my mother Louise were all there. They were all busy doing things and I was not at all certain what they were doing. What I do recall is that they made up a crib with special bedding and they also made up the bed in which Mother and Daddy slept. Aunt Kate and Uncle John, my cousin Amelia and our landlady Mrs. Foeman were also there. In fact when Daddy and Mother finally arrived there was really very little room left for them.

It had to have been several minutes before I had a chance to see my new sister, the girl I had named after three of my favorite people.

Finally Grandma Chambers, my mother's godmother came over and put her hand on my shoulder and said, "Come on let's go and meet your sister!" We walked over to the bed where Mother was now laying down. Mother smiled and pulled back the cover which partially covered the baby's face and head. She had a real beautiful face.

I looked at that face in awe and then I saw.

I blurted out, "Mother, she doesn't have any hair!"

Silence and then laughter filled the house.

Alice Helen Louise had arrived.

Meeting the Champ

Milton Fitch was a member of the Ravaloes. He was one of eight children in the Fitch family. He was also the grandson of William Singleton, a former slave who recruited soldiers for the Union Army during the Civil War. Grandpa Singleton, as many of us called him, was one of my early heroes.

All of Milton's brothers were athletes. They were not just run of the mill jocks, they were good! Collins was a basketball player, Bill was a golfer who initiated an interest in golf among African-Americans in New Haven, Harry was an outstanding baseball, football, basketball and track star. Some people have said that he was as good as my uncle Major (and that means he was really, really good). Roy was outstanding in baseball and basketball. George stood out as a basketball player and boxer. Milton played basketball and Jerry was a standout in basketball. Sis was the only non-athlete in the family. She was a stand out in academics and became a math teacher.

George was a really good boxer and became the light heavyweight champion of New England. He also became one of Joe Louis' sparring partners.

It was during the summer of 1940 that George invited Milton to visit him at Joe's training camp up at Greenwood Lake, New York. Milton who was two years older than I, had graduated from high school a year before me, gone to work, and was purchasing a car.

Milton asked me, Russ McCabe and Morris Simmons to join him on the trip to Greenwood Lake to see his brother George and to meet the champ Joe Louis.

When we arrived at Greenwood Lake we were just in time for lunch. There were quite a few visitors at the camp and I understood that they paid a fee to enter the training camp to watch the champ train. Because we were George's guests we didn't have to pay. George introduced us to some of the other sparring partners. I remember one of the guys was Turkey Thompson. I also found that each member of the sparring partner group and the champ had a nickname. There was Speedboat, Showboat, and Rowboat. It was fun watching the guys horse around.

After lunch we were invited to take a ride out on the lake in the champ's speedboat. The boat was a beauty. It was built of teak wood and had a very powerful engine. Six of us fit comfortably in the boat and the champ put the boat to the test. It didn't take us long to cross the lake and to return. He handled the boat quite well.

Upon our return to the training camp, the champ and Milton's brother George had to prepare for a sparring session. We took our places in the spectator bleachers and awaited the sparring session.

The champ came into the ring with a white towel covering his head and shoulders. His sparring partner, whose name I can't recall, entered the ring. There was a person in the ring - I believe he was Mr. Blackburn who was going to referee the sparring match. The two gladiators donned protective head gear and met with the referee in the center of the ring where he gave them instructions.

Both men returned to their respective corners and stood there until the bell sounded.

Both men came out, touched gloves, and began to box. The champ took a position that we had seen many times in the newspapers – left arm extended, right arm slightly bent, right fist held close to his head. The two men circled each other and then the sparring partner threw a punch which caught the champ on his right upper arm. You could hear the punch land. I turned to say something to Milton. Then I heard a gasp. I looked toward the ring and saw the sparring partner flat on his back in the middle of the ring.

I asked what had happened, and a man in front of me said, "The guy never even saw it coming."

There was a pause in the activities around the boxing ring. After a while we heard a sound of loud laughter and making their way toward the ring was the champ and Milton's brother George. They entered the ring and went through the instructional ritual.

The bell rang and George and the champ moved toward each other. They were smiling and began to jab each other in the ribs. This sort of light action took place during the first three minute round.

During the interval between the rounds the champ and George began to call each other some crazy names. Nothing derogatory or profane but just stupid stuff. I don't know what was said when the two men met at the center of the ring. But all of a sudden George and the champ really began to go at it. The referee separated them several times. During one of the separations the champ slapped George and George hit the champ with a jab and a swing from Lord knows where.

There was silence in the camp. Then someone shouted, "The champ's down." Sure enough the champ was on his back. All of the champ's handlers jumped into the ring to help him to his feet. Someone was yelling at George charging him with hitting the champ with a sucker punch.

Well, the champ got up and walked over to George. They exchanged a few words. I really never found out what was said.

Milton had an additional passenger on the way back to New Haven.

Soldier - Induction

Today is November 11, 2006 and I remember ever so vividly what happened on this day in 1942. Sixty-four years ago.

Eleven months and four days ago the Japanese bombed Pearl Harbor. Our nation is at war and I am twenty years old and about to be sworn into the Army of the United States. I've been drafted. There I stood with several other young and a few middle aged men awaiting the swearing in ceremony that would make us all soldiers.

We had all been given a quick physical examination and with very few exceptions had been pronounced fit to fight for our country. We were a diverse group – white, black, Jew Gentile, Christian, atheist, tall, short, fat, thin. Yes, each of us was a little different than the one who stood next to us.

Unlike many of the others standing there I knew the person standing next to me very intimately. He was my dad. We had been swept up by the draft. The armed services were taking men aged eighteen to forty-five years of age. Dad was forty-three. I was twenty.

At eleven o'clock all of the men in the room were ordered to stand quietly to honor those who had died in previous wars. We were then ordered to raise our right hand to be sworn into the armed forces of the United States. It was exactly 11:05 A.M. on the eleventh day of the eleventh month of 1942.

We were told that we had two weeks to get our affairs in order and to report to the New Haven Railroad Station at 9:00 A.M. the 25th. of November 1942.

This diverse collection of men who would in all likelihood never again come together were now members of the armed forces.

I walked out of the building with my dad. I was not too happy and Dad was obviously upset.

My lack of exuberance stemmed from the fact that I had attempted to volunteer for the army several months earlier and had been turned down because of my color. Dad was upset because he had been told by the president of the Draft Board that he would not be called up because he worked in an essential war industry. The president of the Draft Board was a lodge brother of Dad's and Dad's employer was a gun manufacturer. Dad was a courier between the various offices of the gun manufacturer.

Several days later Dad received word that he was exempted from the service. I don't know who was happier Dad or me.

During the two week period that I had to take care of my affairs I received calls from my Uncle Major, Uncle Billy and my godfather, Uncle Lawson. Each one gave advice on how to survive in the army. None of them had ever served. But the one thing they all advised was to forget my anger about being rejected by the army. They all advised that I make myself a good soldier.

The 25th of November 1942 was a day which I have remembered all these years. This was the day that several hundred men were to be transported to Fort Devens, Massachusetts to begin their military careers.

I arrived at the railway station in the company of my father, mother, Aunt Kate, Uncle John and Uncle Billy. It seemed that each of the inductees, as we were then called, brought along a large contingent of family members.

By 8:50 that morning the station was packed with people. At about 8:45 there was a call for everyone to be quiet so that all could hear a speech by the Mayor of the City of New Haven. I can't remember a word uttered by the Mayor other than, "God bless each of you." At this point we were ordered to board the train.

As I turned to join the other inductees my mother began to cry and my dad embraced me and kissed me on the cheek and said "Be careful boy!" Uncle John and Uncle Billy embraced me and shook my hand. Each one of them handed me a ten dollar bill. Aunt Katie gave a big hug and kissed me. She also handed me a paper bag and whispered in my ear that it was a special package that would make the train ride a little shorter.

I boarded the train and found a seat with some of my buddies. We hadn't been seated for more than five minutes when I heard the conductor shout, "Board, All Aboard." The train jerked and then began to move. As I looked about I couldn't find a dry eye among the brave young men seated in my car. But then my vision was blurred from my own tears.

The train moved slowly away from New Haven and I noticed that most of the trees had lost their leaves. I also noted for the first time that there were some men in uniform walking down the aisle of our car. These men wore arm bands imprinted with the letters MP. One of my buddies said, "These guys must be the new conductors. As the two soldiers passed one said, "Any beer or liquor must be disposed of now!" None of us had any liquor so we weren't concerned. Shortly after they passed I reached down for Aunt Katie's package, picked it up, looked in the bag and saw an Italian submarine sandwich. I removed it from the bag and felt the bag's bottom and realized that there was a bottle inside. Indeed it was a bottle of 4 Roses whiskey.

A quick glance told me that the soldiers had gone into the next car. I opened the bottle, took a little swig and passed the bottle to my buddies. Each of them took a swig and passed the bottle to the people in the next seat. I don't know how far the bottle went but as Aunt Katie said when she handed me the bag, "This will make your trip shorter."

Death of a Soldier

I turned on the television this morning and was greeted with the news that an American soldier who had been a captive of Al Qaeda had been found dead. My reaction was one of anger at his cowardly captors. These pseudo-humans, who claim to be adherents to Islam, have done nothing but prove themselves to be liars and cowards. A soldier is trained to fight his enemy and if necessary to die in battle. But to die at the hands of liars and cowards is an abomination.

Though I never faced an enemy soldier in combat, I was trained to do so and therefore trained to die.

Many years ago I was given the honor of being the escort guard to a fallen soldier. I believe I was selected because I was articulate and made a fairly good military presence.

My orders were to accompany and guard the remains of a fallen sergeant. His remains were to travel from Massachusetts to California. I had never before traveled across the United States and certainly never had been given such a great responsibility. The thought of handling such an awesome task was somewhat frightening to me.

My first shock was receiving the sergeant's remains from the civilian mortician. The mortician handed me the travel documents and instructions for handling the coffin during transit.

I had never heard of a hermetically sealed coffin. I had no idea how important it was that the coffin had to be handled very carefully. Mishandling might cause the seal to be breeched and thereby cause a rapid deterioration of the body.

This was of particular importance since we were traveling during the month of August.

We boarded the train in the early evening. I boarded a Pullman sleeping car after supervising the sergeant's boarding in a box car. There was no air conditioning in the box car; in fact it was quite stuffy.

The train got underway and we began our journey toward the setting sun. This was my first time riding on a train with sleeping cars. Most of the passengers were military. I seemed to be the only person of color in my car. This was brought to my attention by the sleeping car porter. He came through the train and announced that the berths were ready. When he got to my seat he tapped me on the shoulder and motioned for me to follow him. When we got to the end of the car he held out his hand to shake mine and told me that since I was the only colored soldier in his car he was going to look out for me. I told him that I knew Willis Moore. Before I could continue he exclaimed, "You know Willie?"

I told the porter of my relationship with Mr. Moore. He in turn told me that he was only going as far as Chicago but that he would pass me off to the man who would take his place and I would be looked out for all the way to Sacramento.

The trip across the United States was exciting especially since I had a "team" of expert tour guides and wonderful guardians. My porter friends pointed out points of interest such as the Mississippi River which we crossed in Minnesota and the Great Salt Lake in Utah. They directed me to great eating places when the train had long layovers. One of the most exciting parts of the trip was being awakened very early on the morning of my last day on the trip and told to come to the rear platform of the train.

It was just dawn, the sun had begun to rise and as I stepped out onto the platform I was greeted by the most awesome sight. I believe I gasped at it. We were coming down from out of the mountains. I looked out and all that I could see and smell were magnificent, stately pine trees. Mixed with the smell of the pine was the smell of steel, hot steel. The smell of steel came from the wheels of the train as brakes were applied as the train descended the mountain.

The conductor told me to look toward the front of the train. It was amazing to see the front of the train now being pulled by two engines going around the sharp curves around the mountains. This was a sight that I shall never forget. Nor will I ever forget the distinctive combinations of smells of pine and burning steel.

Several hours later we arrived in Sacramento. I was quite excited and relieved. The sergeant had finally arrived home. When I stepped down from the train I went immediately to the box car to oversee the unloading of the sergeant's body.

The baggage handlers were very respectful of the body which was draped with the flag of the United States. People on the platform stopped and gazed. Some held their hand over their heart, others saluted as the make shift caisson passed by.

I wondered, as I walked by the curious, but respectful civilian observers, just what were they thinking. I wondered if any of them had sons or brothers in the military. I wondered if any of them cared whether the caisson carried a black man, or a white man, a red or yellow man. I wondered what I was going to say to the sergeant's survivors.

When we arrived at the loading platform I saw the black hearse and standing beside it two gentlemen dressed in black. One of them came over to me offered his hand, introduced himself and asked if I had the official transit documents. I handed the papers over to the representative of the funeral home and then observed the transfer from wagon to hearse. I was then told that the sergeant's survivors were at the funeral home awaiting his arrival.

The funeral director then opened the door on the passenger side of the hearse and gestured to me to enter and be seated. We were soon underway and the sergeant would be reunited with his loved ones.

Klumpf Funeral Chapel, our destination, was reached in a few minutes. The hearse was driven to the rear of the chapel. An attendant opened the door for me and in a soft voice informed me that the survivors were waiting for me in the viewing parlor. I walked alongside the attendant through a dimly lighted hallway, passing several well appointed rooms. We finally reached a rather large room with several chairs and I saw two women seated at the front of the room.

I walked to the front of the room and stopped in front of the two women. In my very best military manner I bowed, held out my hand and introduced myself. Both women were small attractive women but it was obvious both had been grieving. Their eyes were red and troubled. I couldn't help what I did next. Leaning down I gathered the two women together and embraced the two of them. This was of course not military behavior but when I saw these two lovely, lonely women I just had to hold them and protect them.

When I gathered these two tiny women I too cried. I really don't know why – I didn't even know the sergeant. I was here to represent the Army of the United States and here I, a sergeant of that army, stood crying like a baby.

The funeral director came in and broke the spell of the moment by calling me aside. He informed me that the casket's hermetic seal had been breached and that some deterioration had taken place. He said that the remains would not be ready for viewing for two days. He suggested that I convince the two ladies (the sergeant's mother and aunt) to go to the cemetery to select a grave.

It was difficult to convince the two women to leave the funeral chapel. I took it upon myself to tell them the truth. They both thanked me and we left in a limousine to go to the cemetery.

We were shown several plots but only one satisfied the two sisters. It was a beautiful tree shaded hillside plot which I believe would have been selected by the sergeant had he been able.

As we were leaving the cemetery the sergeant's mother asked if I would stay at her home until after the funeral service. I gratefully accepted. The sergeant's mother and aunt lived together. I learned that they had moved to California from Kansas less than a year ago. They had no close friends and in fact had not even joined a church.

The day of the funeral stands out in my mind even today. We were picked up at the house at about 12:30 P.M. I had eaten a fine breakfast after awakening from a good night's sleep. The limousine took us to the funeral parlor and we entered at 1:00 P.M. to the sound of muted organ music.

There must have been 50 chairs in the room. Six of those chairs were occupied when we walked in. No one stood or acknowledged our presence. We took our seats and the music stopped. A gentleman stood and announced that he was reverend somebody or other. I never did hear the name. He went on to speak of the virtues of being a soldier and dying in battle. He spoke about the history of great military heroes.

The sergeant's mother and aunt sobbed softly. Sobbing sounds emanated from the four or five seats that we occupied. The reverend completed his eulogy, came over and shook the hands of the sergeant's mother and aunt. He shook my hand and asked if I was a relative.

I heard sounds at the rear of the room and looked around to see an eight man detail of soldiers. They marched in two columns to the front, saluted and formed around the coffin; they lifted it and walked out with the sergeant. We followed and watched the sergeant being placed in the hearse.

The trip to the cemetery was very quiet. We arrived at the cemetery and I spotted two army personnel carriers parked near the grave site. The pallbearer detail went about its duties. A military chaplain said prayers. A detail of riflemen fired the traditional salute and Taps was played. I presented the flag which had covered the sergeant's coffin to his mother and then said goodbye.

Mrs. Green, she was the sergeant's mother, grasped my hand and thanked me for bringing her son Al home. Alfred was the sergeant's name. She pulled me close and whispered in my ear, "When you talk to your mother tell her that when she prays for you to come home be sure to tell God to bring you home alive and in good health."

She then went on – "He answered my prayers. He sent Al home."

The funeral director gave me a ride to the railroad station and I found that I had a four hour wait. I called my mother in New York.

I then read a local newspaper and saw a story about Master Sergeant Alfred Green, a sergeant in a field artillery battalion who had been killed suddenly when electrocuted by lightening when it struck a tree near his tent on the range near Wellfleet, Massachusetts.

Joe Louis

Freddie Martin was the officers' mess steward. Freddie was what one might call a soldier with the golden touch. Our company had only three officers and when we were in the field the officers usually ate with the men. However when we were in barracks there was an officers' table and Freddie served that table which he called the "officer's mess."

There was no position in our company table of organization (T.O.) called Officer's Mess Steward. Since our officers (all of whom were African – American) were not "welcomed" at the base officers club. Freddie convinced our C.O. that our officers should have an officers' mess. He also pointed out that since he had the distinction of having been the head waiter at an exclusive men's club in Richmond, Virginia he could provide our officers service unequaled any place on the base. This Freddie did. He even donned a white coat to wait on the officers' table.

Freddie took on other responsibilities such as doing the officers' laundry and cleaning up the officers' quarters. Freddie had it made because the First Sergeant took him off the regular duty roster. Freddie also partook of the officers' rations (which they paid for).

I was placed on special assignment as Special Services Non-Com and worked out of the Post Arena. One of my first assignments was to setup a boxing show that involved men from my company and challengers from other units on the base.

Ed Deal (Sgt.) was the Special Services Non-Com for the base. He took me under his wing and guided my actions for the period of time I was attached to his office.

I walked into the office one day and Ed told me to sit down because he had something important to tell me. The something important was that he had just received word that the World Heavyweight Champion Joe Louis was coming to the base for an exhibition. He also said that Middleweight Champ Sugar Ray Robinson would also be coming. My assignment was to setup their itinerary for the day which by the way was the day that my boxing show was to take place.

I had about two weeks to get things moving. Ed promised to contact the Caucasian units and since my company was the only non-white unit on the base my task was to get volunteers to participate in the show. We had some very good boxers and a large number of "fighters". Fighter is the operative word here. Our guys were real fighters and when they heard that "The Champ" was going to be present I had more than enough volunteers to fill a sixteen bout card.

The details about setting up the boxing show are interesting but not essential to be spelled out here. The fact was Ed had some difficulty getting enough white volunteers to appear on the card. The reader must keep in mind this was a segregated army, even in the state of Massachusetts.

Well the day came and Ed, the Post Special Services Officer, the Post Commander and I awaited the arrival of the "Champions" - Joe and Sugar Ray and their entourage. When they arrived a Colonel Fields stepped off the bus and spoke to the Post Commander and Special Services Officer. The SSO summoned Ed and me and told us that Joe, Ray and the other boxers were now my responsibility. You must continue to remember that this was a segregated army.

I had been given permission to use a staff car from the post motor pool. I was also given responsibility for a weapons carrier and a driver. The weapons carrier was to carry the rest of the entourage and equipment. One of the members of the entourage was a guy by the name "Turkey" Thompson. He was the champ's sparring partner.

When all of the introductions had been made, I took the champs over to "my" staff car and with the weapons carrier following, started the drive to my company area. This is where the champs and their entourage were to spend the day.

Our company area was distinguished by the type of barracks in which we were housed. The majority of the base consisted of two story white barracks. We, the mighty 722nd, Medical Sanitation Company, were housed in tar paper covered barracks at the back end of the post.

But, we were all well disciplined and resourceful men. We developed the area into a showcase. We had a lot of time since our mission did not seem to be clear to the army. So, we landscaped, we embellished, we established ownership to what some might have called a slum in the civilian world.

On the way over to my company area I asked Joe Louis if his friends still called him "Speedboat". He looked quizzically at me and asked where I had picked up that information. I told him that I was a friend of George Fitch who had been one of his sparring partners. He nodded and said something to the effect that George was a good guy. I didn't tell the Champ that I had been present at his training camp when George had knocked him down. I told Joe that he had taken a group of us in his motorboat across Greenwood Lake. This established a good rapport between Joe and me.

Our company commander Captain Hudson and the other officers, Lieutenants Thompson and Tyner were introduced to the "champs" and we went about the business of setting up an exhibition for the troops.

That afternoon Joe indicated he wanted to go into town and see some ladies. We won't go into detail on this matter.

When we arrived back at the post late that afternoon we prepared to go to dinner.

Now, we get back to Freddie Martin, the officers' mess steward. As noted before, the officers' mess consisted of three officers. Today was a special day. Today the mess hall of the 722nd Medical Sanitation Company became integrated.

The post commander, the post special services officer, and Col. Fields all showed up for dinner. I later learned that the base commander had taken it upon himself to invite the others to join our officers for dinner.

The non-commissioned officers in my unit had decided when they heard that the Champ was coming to chip in and buy steaks for a special meal for our heroes Joe and Sugar Ray. We occasionally did something like this and were proud of the fact that our little 127 man unit had an outstanding kitchen. Sgt. Blackwell was part of our sergeants group and saw to it that we got great food.

I'm sure that you have gotten a sense of the excitement that permeated the environs of our mess hall. The sergeants had made a deal with Freddy that he would serve the non-com table after serving the officers. He jumped at the deal.

The mess hall had been magically transformed to the dining hall. There were two large hand lettered banners welcoming the champs. All of the troops were dressed in class A uniforms. Our C.O. welcomed all the visiting officers and the champions.

Dinner was served family style with the exception of the officers and non-com tables.

Then Freddie made his entrance. He carried a thirty inch aluminum tray with several plates and headed to the officers' table. He served the officers with a flourish and then headed back to the kitchen.

After a few minutes delay Freddie reappeared and headed toward the non-com table. He was carrying the same tray. He set the tray down and placed two large bowls of beef stew on the table. Sergeant Blackwell, the mess sergeant whispered loudly, "Freddie where are the steaks?" Freddie looked confused and said, "I served them to the officers."

The loud talk and laughter continued in the mess hall. But, the non-coms table had a group of dour faced men and Freddie whose confused look turned to a terrified mask opened his mouth but nothing came out.

Joe Louis broke the spell and said to me in a voice loud enough for the non-com table to hear – "Hey man I love steak and gravy". I started to say something but he continued – "and potatoes, and onions and gravy." The table cracked up.

Freddy Martin never lived down that day. All of the non-coms when they came upon Freddy would say – "Where's the steak?"

Up the Gangplank

Television serves as a catalyst to my mind as I try to recall the many things that have happened during the course of my life.

Today I turned on my television to view Queen Elizabeth's arrival at the White House. I viewed the welcoming ceremony and was impressed by the pomp and the martial music. As I listened to the music a distant memory emerged, one that was deeply buried in my past.

It was March 1944 and my unit had been ordered to overseas duty. We entrained to Camp Stoneman in California. We had undergone our final training and were psychologically ready to face the enemy.

Orders came down from higher headquarters for us to report for embarkation. We were a proud bunch. We had reconciled ourselves to the fact that we were part of an army that was segregated by race. We had determined that no one was going to make us, as a unit, feel inferior.

Our unit had been issued clothing while we were still at Fort Devins in Massachusetts. There was no question in our collective minds that we were going to Alaska. Our new issue consisted of parkas, heavy snow boots, heavy two piece long underwear and fur mittens. Also a part of our training included learning how to use snowshoes and also how to camouflage ourselves in snow. We were certain that the only place we could be sent just had to be the Aleutians. We were ready!!!

We arrived at the port of embarkation sometime about midday.

Our officers ordered the platoon sergeants to form up their platoon in columns of twos. There were several other soldiers at the port and they had begun to board the ship - The Henry J. Austin.

The military band struck up stirring marches and the troops with heads held high marched up the gangplank. Our company awaited its turn. We waited and waited. After a two and a half hour wait our commanding officer called us to attention. We immediately stood proudly at attention. We were to be the last to board the ship. The echoes of the martial music rang in our ears. Our commanding officer delayed giving the command to march. The gangplank cleared and the band stopped playing. The command Forward March came, the band played an introductory fanfare and we started up the gangplank.

The band leader waited until the first section of the first platoon had gotten about halfway up and then gave the downbeat and the band started to play "Bye Bye Blackbird."

There was a moment of disbelief – a look passed from one soldier to another. We stopped marching. A command came from below. The command was from one of the port officers. Keep moving, keep moving.

One of our men yelled out "Bullshit". Several other expletives came from our men and finally one of our guys threw his helmet into the band. Several more followed and some of the men started to turn to go back down to get to the band.

The music stopped and the band now in disarray moved toward the shed.

A company of MPs came onto the scene with truncheons at the ready. They were ready to crack heads. So were we.

Our captain yelled above the din. But no one paid much attention. Our first sergeant pushed his way to the base of the gangplank. He had been a wrestler in college. He met the leading MP and pushed him back. He then yelled "Men of the Seven-Deuce-Deuce get back on this gangplank or face me later.

We all respected William T. and the men reluctantly returned to the gangplank and began the upward walk. First Sergeant William T. walked down to where the thrown helmets lay on the dock. He picked them up and turned and mounted the gangplank.

The ship left the dock shortly afterward. We sailed under the Golden Gate Bridge with no sound other than the ship cutting through the water.

No pomp. No martial music. No nothing!

Oh yes, the first sergeant returned the retrieved helmets to their owners. This was easily done since their names were printed inside each helmet.

The General's Crapper

I guess I should be happy that I've lived for such a long time. There is no guess about it. I am truly happy to have experienced so much of what the world has to offer, some good – some bad, but all very enriching.

Many more of my generation served in the armed forces during the Second World War and the Korean conflict. We are described as the great generation. We produced many heroes.

Among the young men with whom I grew up and personally knew, there were two bronze stars, one Silver Star, and a Congressional Medal of Honor recipient. Those men had all placed their lives on the line during the height of battle. I don't know the details but a recent news story reminded me that the Congressional Medal of Honor winner and I had been in the same second grade class. The other medal recipients and I used to play together and had renewed our friendship after the war. In fact these guys were brothers and it was not surprising that they were heroes.

The fact that these men became heroes probably emanated from our early days as boys in the neighborhood.

There is probably no rationale for me to mention that the three brothers were African-American and the other was Caucasian. His name was Bobby and as I recall had been a real nice kid who could hold his own in the neighborhood.

The three brothers, Jim, a lieutenant in the infantry served in Italy; Al, who was a twin to George, served in France and Burma respectively.

Jim earned a medal in Italy, Al at the Battle of the Bulge, and George in Burma.

Now these four guys are just an example of the heroic nature of our generation. But I represent another side. I too served in the Army of the United States and eventually became a sergeant. I served my country in the Southwest Pacific and in the Philippines. Though I earned no medals for bravery in combat, I did serve in a unit that received a meritorious unit award. This meant that the men in my unit were authorized to wear a meritorious unit patch on the sleeve of our uniforms.

When I returned home after the war in January 1946 I proudly wore my uniform for about two weeks. A lot of returnees couldn't wait to get into civilian clothes. But, I was not that anxious to change into civvies primarily because most of the clothes that I had left behind no longer fit and I didn't have money enough to buy new clothes.

There was one other factor that kept me in uniform and that was the attention it drew from the ladies. That in itself was a real bonus. "Oh my," they would exclaim when they saw my single row of ribbons. And those who spotted the meritorious unit wreath on my sleeve just knew that I was a hero.

Now believe me, I never declared that I was a hero. I would just explain when asked about the wreath that I was a member of a meritorious service unit.

I have no idea what went through people's minds when they heard meritorious service unit. Whatever it was it sure paid off in drinks and kisses.

Very few people asked what it was that my unit had done to garner such an honor and I never volunteered. For the few that asked I told the truth.

My unit was the 722nd Medical Sanitation Company. We were a unique group of mostly young, intelligent, black men. We were unique in that the unit had 125 men representing at least 12 states. We also came from diverse backgrounds. We had college graduates, high school graduates and those who had attended grammar school or no school at all. We were farmers, lumber jacks, fishermen, factory workers, gamblers, hustlers, and preachers. We were indeed a diverse group.

The men of the 722nd were a proud group of men, all of whom were ready to carry out whatever missions were set for us to carry out. Because of our pride and the quality of our work we were often given tasks that were not set forth in our mission. We drove motor convoys, loaded and unloaded ships, stood guard duty and on one occasion sent men to face enemy soldiers.

Our unit was supposed to provide support to hospitals. We were to provide such services as handling disposal of waste, rodent and pest control. We dug miles of drainage ditches to get rid of mosquito larvae.

Our men were trained to do lab work and to work as ward attendants. I believe that our technical training came about because our first commanding officer Captain Crockett, a medical officer from Washington D.C., insisted that his men's training be commensurate with their education. So those of us who had college or high school education received excellent training. We also were trained to do the scut work. Above all we were trained in basic infantry skills. We learned to use infantry weapons such as M1's, A2 carbines, Browning and Thompson machine guns, 45 caliber pistols and automatics, hand to hand combat training including the use of the trench knife. Some of us were sent to special training schools. I attended school to learn how to become an expert in camouflage. I also learned to make and use Molotov Cocktails and anti-personnel devices. We were well trained.

Trained for what? is the question we asked ourselves. We were treated shabbily while in the states. But when there was need for a sharp marching group we were called.

Once we arrived overseas we were assigned to do engineering work such as road repair, ditch digging and whatever else needed doing.

Our first overseas assignment was with a field hospital. We were given mosquito control around the hospital (27th Field Hospital). The task was approached with all of the expertise that our training provided us. We dug drainage ditches and sprayed the area. Some of our men also dug out areas for latrines which we later sanitized by pouring a mix of gasoline and used motor oil over the latrine waste and igniting it. This process eliminated flies and kept smell to a minimum.

We became expert latrine diggers and builders. This expertise leads me back to the meritorious service unit award.

Several months after our arrival in New Guinea we were ordered to move north to Hollandia which was soon to become the headquarters for General Mc Arthur.

Our unit was given the responsibility of digging the pit for the general's latrine and to build the throne (toilet seats) and the housing to protect the users from the elements and whatever else. The throne was built by our unit carpenter Sgt. Henderson. It was a six seater, made of teak wood. It was a sight to behold! I really don't know if the general ever used it but it was certainly a work of art.

Our commanding officer received a letter from the base commander that our unit had been designated a Meritorious

Service Unit and as such the men of the unit were authorized to wear the wreath patch.

So, I want to make it known to all that though I received no medals for bravery in action I and the men of the proud 722nd Medical Sanitation Company did earn distinction for building a latrine for General McArthur.

Heroes

I've been looking at television and listening to varied commentary emanating from the various venues which television opens for us. I took great interest in the commentary regarding the wounded warriors who fought in Iraq.

Today's comments had to do with the lack of proper oversight of the facilities to which recovering wounded veterans were assigned in Washington, D.C. Pictures of some of the quarters to which the veterans were assigned were shown and needless to say were quite dramatic.

Well, I too am a veteran of a war, a war that took place many years ago. That war was the era in which I grew up. One cannot compare wars and the horrors one experiences as a result thereof.

I sometimes think of the time I spent as a soldier on active duty. I spent about three years on active duty. Approximately one and a half years of that time overseas.

My experiences as a soldier were invaluable and as I noted earlier this is the place that shaped my life from boyhood to manhood. This was the place where my early experiences in life were tested. This was where my beliefs such as they were, were tested. Truth, inner strength, faith, courage, love, fear each of these beliefs were tested and often times stressed to the limits of human endurance.

I was trained as all soldiers to follow orders and to work in concert with others to accomplish completion of a task. As all soldiers I was also trained during wartime to kill or be killed.

Now heroes are generally seen as persons whose beliefs have been tested to the extreme and who have lived or died by the admonition of "kill or be killed." The people who are seen as heroes stand out above all others by virtue of the circumstance in which they find themselves at any given moment. During a war that circumstance usually involves combat. It involves facing the enemy and prevailing in some sort of confrontation.

I am one of those soldiers who never confronted a Japanese or German soldier on the battlefield. I saw some Japanese, German and Italian prisoners of war. In fact had a chance to talk to some of them. But never did I confront one with a fear for my life.

In January 1946 I was returning home from overseas duty. Our plane stopped in Dallas, Texas to refuel and to allow those soldiers aboard to eat. There were three African-Americans aboard. I also had responsibility for the meal tickets. As the group approached the airport restaurant a civilian police officer confronted the group and informed us that the group could enter the restaurant but that the "colored boys" would have to go around back.

I stepped forward and said that I held the meal tickets and that no one would eat unless we all ate. The police officer bellied up to me and said, "I said no colored can eat in the restaurant." Without pause, I called the man a cracker "M – F."

I was wrong! The police officer drew his revolver and pointed it at my head. I told him to go ahead and shoot. His hand shook and my gut began to quiver. He didn't shoot.

Well, that was the circumstance in which I found myself in January 1946 thousands of miles from any battlefield confronting an enemy who tested my courage and my beliefs.

Yes, heroes are perceived by many as persons whose courage and belief have been tested to an extreme.

When I related this story to some of my friends a few years ago their response was "You always were a damn fool."

March 29, 2007

I received a telephone call from my sister Alyce last night. She called to let me now that she had arrived home after a week's stay in Florida. I noted that she seemed a bit talky, which is quite unusual for her. She finally told me that she had some bad news to tell me.

It's a strange thing but somehow I had a foreboding of something for a few days. I couldn't put my finger on it, but I sensed that something was amiss.

She finally said, "Tim has passed." "So?" you ask. Who is Tim? Well Tim was one of my buddies. He and I met in the Philippines during the war (i.e. WWII)). He was a replacement for one of our men who was sent back to the states.

Tim was a tall, thin, light-complexioned fellow and was obviously quite nervous. He jumped down from the back of the truck in which he had been traveling.

He had been assigned to my section which was a part of the first platoon. I introduced myself and told him to pick up his duffle bag and follow me. It was about 8:00 P.M. and the men in my section were sitting in the large tent going about various busy work.

As we walked through the tent I turned and saw a look of consternation of Tim's face. When we arrived at his cot he turned to me and commented. "They told me this was a non-combat outfit." I replied that we were a non-combat unit assigned to a general hospital. He then asked why the men were sharpening bayonets, field knives and oiling pistols.

I remember laughing and telling him that the men were preparing to go to town for the evening.

Tim fit in quite well. A couple of days following his arrival there was an open boxing contest. This meant that anyone could throw out a challenge to the group and the person taking the challenge would pick up the unused pair of boxing gloves. Several of the guys moved into the circle and sparred with the challenger.

To my surprise Tim picked up the gloves and stepped into the circle. Two of the spectators moved into the circle and helped Tim put on the gloves and tied them up. The challenger, a fellow from Washington, D.C. (can't remember his name), began to talk about whipping some fresh butt. Tim replied loudly proclaiming that in order to whip butt you had to catch it. With that declaration Corporal Turner called the two combatants to the middle of the circle for instructions. Both men appeared anxious. They touched gloves and began to box. Tim got in two left jabs and dodged a wild right aimed at his head. Then the fun began.

Tim got in a couple of punches and then began to back peddle. His opponent kept pushing forward but couldn't catch Tim. Tim showed unusual footwork and was surprisingly adept at keeping his opponent off balance. The match lasted just three minutes. At the end of the match the observers let out a loud cheer for the new guy. Tim was now an accepted member of the 722nd.

I tell the story about Tim because it exemplified the character of the man. Tim was a graduate of Manhattan College in New York. He was a native New Yorker and aspired to become a physician. In fact he had been accepted as a student at Howard University Medical School. I got to know Tim pretty well over the several months we served together in the Philippines in 1945.

It wasn't until 1951 that I came across Tim once more. My friend Eddie and I were walking up Dixwell Avenue and he mentioned that there was a new doctor in town. We continued walking and talking and Eddie said the new doctor's name was Timpson. I told Eddie that I had served overseas with a guy named Timpson. In fact his name was Richard Timpson and he was from New York. We decided to stop and visit the new doctor's office.

We arrived at the doctor's office, walked in and asked the nurse as to whether the doctor was available. She inquired as to our problem. I told her that I was an old friend of the doctor. With that the door to the inner office opened and a tall, thin, smiling young man in a white coat walked out.

He approached me with his hand thrust out and said, "I would know that voice anywhere. How're you doing Sarge?" With that he turned to his receptionist and said, " This was my sergeant in the Philippines".

Yes Tim and I became very close friends. We had a number of similar interests in sports, politics and many other areas.

I'm so sorry that he didn't live to fulfill his wish to live to be one hundred and be shot by a jealous husband.

Post War

January, 1946 was the month I returned home from overseas duty. I had spent several months between New Guinea and the Philippines. There is much to write about during this period in my life. But I really want to write about the period after the war.

When I arrived back in Connecticut there were no brass bands, no parades, and no welcoming speeches. There was just my dad waiting on the platform at the New Haven Union Terminal.

I had called Dad from a pay phone in Pennsylvania Station in New York. Our plane had landed at Newark Airport at about 10:00 P.M. and we were taken by bus to the train station. We boarded the Washington to Boston train at about 11:00 P.M. and arrived at Penn Station, New York at about 11:30 P.M. I knew that the train had to stop in New Haven to change engines.

My welcoming committee was standing on the platform when the train pulled into New Haven at about 1:30 A.M. It wasn't difficult to find Dad. He was the only one standing on the platform.

My arrival in New Haven was a far cry from my departure on 25 November 1942. There was no crowd – only Dad. I stepped off the train and started to walk toward Dad. He stood there with a smile that was so warm it heated up that cold January morning. We embraced. I don't remember saying anything. We just held each other. It reminded me of a night some twenty-two years before when Dad let me sit on his shoulders. That night I looked up and said, "Daddy, there's a light in the sky."

As I embraced Dad I looked up and saw a bright star. There was a light in the sky.

Organizer

Labor Day is a special day for many people especially those who work in the labor unions.

A few months after returning home from the war I registered for college and found a job. This was the pattern that many vets followed since the G. I. Bill made it possible to attend college.

Getting a job was a necessity in order to pay my room and board even though I was living with my dad and his wife and family.

The job was interesting in that it was in a non-union factory. I was hired as a drill press operator on the 4:00 P.M. to 12:00 midnight shift. My co-workers were all Caucasian and primarily Italian. Many spoke little English. They were nice to me and encouraged me to do well on the job. They showed me a few tricks on how to meet any work quota. I told them that I was a full time student and a veteran. This stood me in good stead especially when I told them I had served in the Pacific.

I had been at the factory a few weeks when I was approached by a fellow while outside on my lunch break. He asked if I was familiar with the efforts being made to unionize the factory. I told him I was aware of it through some circulars that had been given to me when I left work a few times. He asked if I was in favor of unions, a question which I answered affirmatively. I was then invited to attend a meeting to learn more about efforts being made to organize the factory.

I attended the meeting and met a number of other workers all of whom worked on the day shift (i.e. 8 A.M. to 4 P.M.). I learned that the factory bosses had forbidden any organizing activities in or around the factory under the threat of firing. I listened carefully and decided that I would become involved by trying to recruit workers on my shift to sign up for a union.

I left the meeting with a bag filled with circulars and cards.

When I arrived at work the following Monday I waited until lunch break and began to approach my fellow workers with circulars and signature cards. I say I approached my fellow workers but I should note here that I approached two fellow workers and before I could talk to any more, the workers began to converse in Italian. As I approached other workers I began to hear the word "Communista." Any attempts to speak to my fellow workers fell upon deaf ears.

After a few days of trying to converse with my fellow workers I decided it would be better if I didn't push any more. This decision was made when I discovered a number of unfinished pieces of work in my finished work barrel.

I punched my time card at about 12:05 A.M. and began to walk home. The weather was good and I felt really fine having just received my pay check. Usually I walked to the center of town which was about 10 minutes from the factory. I had taken this walk many times and never had any problems. Tonight was to be different.

Just about two blocks past the factory I was grabbed from behind and lifted off my feet. I am or at least at that time stood six feet two inches tall and weighed about 200 pounds. I was in good physical shape. Before I could react I was thrown to the ground. It was then I realized that there were three persons involved. Two of them held me down and the third person addressed me.

I recall him saying to me, "You f------g communist bastard, we're going to break your f------g jaw so you can't try to give that communist s---- to the guys in your shop. We are all war veterans and we are not going to let some smart black communist bastard f---k up our people."

I guess I should have been flattered that they considered me a "smart black communist bastard." I was too scared to be anything but scared. Having served for three years in the Army of the United States I recognized that I was in a difficult position and was dealing with men who had also spent time serving the country.

Trying to fight back seemed to be futile. The guys holding me down were strong. My mind kept going back to something my dad had told me years ago. He told me that when faced with a situation which meant you were going to get an "ass whipping" you had better prepare for the pain or try to outsmart your opponent. Ideally your opponent had to have the ability to reason. If he was too smart he would see through your ploy. If he was too stupid he would probably just ignore anything you might say. He had to be just smart enough to listen.

My hope was that the spokesperson for this group was just smart enough.

I addressed the group by telling them that I was also a veteran and had served in the Pacific. This elicited no response. I went on to say that I had worked in a field hospital and had helped treat soldiers who had been seriously injured in tanks. I described seeing soldiers who had been burned over almost every inch of their body. I told them of hearing soldiers crying out to be shot because they couldn't endure the pain of their wounds.

Suddenly the spokesman said, "Shut-up!" I kept talking and he said that nothing I had said had anything to do with what I was doing at the factory. He said that I was taking advantage of a group of illiterate immigrants. This gave me a chance to talk about the pain these poor immigrants were suffering. The fact was that they were earning less than anyone else in the city.

The spokesman signaled the guy holding my legs to let go. He then leaned over me and said "I guess you understand pain?" My head nod answered the question. He asked if I was a communist which was answered in the negative. I told him I was still a reservist and had joined so that I could fight against the world-wide conquest by Russia.

With this revelation he signaled the man holding my arms to let go. The spokesman whom I found out later was the brother of a former high school classmate. We talked about another half hour and I left with the agreement that I would not pass out any more circulars. The spokesperson whose name turned out to be Tony told me he had been in the Marines and had served in the Pacific and could relate to what I had said about the wounded soldiers that I had seen.

The four of us walked to the center of town.

I arrived home at about 2:30 A. M and gave some thought to what had happened. There was a large question in my mind. That question was, "Are you working for a communist organization? It didn't take me long to find an answer. The answer was "Yes!"

My rationale for agreeing to help organize the union was not politically inspired. I was truly concerned that the factory by which we were employed paid the lowest hourly rate of any of the factories in town. I also learned that the owners and management dealt ruthlessly with the workers. They did this by threatening to fire on the spot anyone involved in union activity. They also summarily fired anyone who failed to produce his quota of work. This was exceptionally cruel since work quotas might change day to day.

I wondered why I had not been fired. The answer came from one of the few workers who still talked to me. He told me in very simple language. He said the word was out that I was to have been beaten up and have my jaw broken. He said everyone in the factory knew about it. The beating was intended to give a message to all the workers. The fact that I showed up for work the next afternoon gave rise to some speculation that either I was protected by God or that I was slated for worse things, like getting killed.

I finished my shift at midnight and left the factory. As I walked down the street toward the scene of the previous night's debacle I moved to the middle of the street. I was also carrying a metal rod that was about 18 inches in length and about an inch wide. I passed the site of the previous night's incident without any problem.

As I continued walking I sensed that I was being followed. I refused to turn around and look, but I quickened my step. I made it to the center of town without incident, caught my bus and went home.

The next morning which was Saturday I called one of my friends and told him of the incident. He told me that his advice was to quit the job and give my full attention to my college classes. He also told me that the factory where I worked had a bad reputation. He said several beatings had taken place in and around the factory.

That following Monday morning I went to the factory's personnel office, quit and collected one day's pay.

As I was leaving the personnel office I noticed a work crew digging a trench in front of the building. One of the crew gave me a mock salute – it was Tony.

Well, hardly a Labor Day passes that I don't think about my experience as a labor union organizer. Over the years I have had a hand in helping to organize two union locals, but with far less drama.

Politics – Politics

One of my college classmates wrote the following "The Man the 19th Ward Should Have Run!" Reflecting back to that period I don't think he was correct.

I opted to follow another path in the political arena.

Shortly after returning to New Haven at war's end I began talking to other returning veterans and discovered that we all had similar concerns. We were concerned about employment, housing, education, health matters and general acceptance by the community.

I happened to mention my personal concerns to an old childhood friend named James Curry. Jim felt that we needed to voice our concerns with other vets in a public forum.

There was a community center known as the Dixwell Community House where matters of community interest were aired.

Now the reader must understand that both Jim and I were aware of the American Legion, Veterans of Foreign Wars and other groups set up to help veterans. The problem was that no one seemed to reach out to the returning African-American vets, so we set about setting up our own veterans group. We met at the Dixwell Community House (Q-House) and brought to life the New Haven Veterans Committee.

The group met monthly and discussed issues such as veterans housing, civil service jobs and health issues. Some members of the group raised questions as to why white veterans were being given preference to buy newly built houses at a state subsidized mortgage rate of 2%. Another question raised was why white vets seemed to be getting post office jobs and African Americans were not even notified when exams were to be given.

Some of the Afro-American vets complained that when they inquired about veteran housing the banks claimed to have no information and directed the vets back to the V.A. or whatever agency had referred them.

It took us awhile to understand that we were being given the run-around and that we needed to take some action. We decided to seek help from people in the political arena and so we went to the alderman in our district. He assured us that he would look into our problem and get back to us.

We waited several days and heard nothing. Jim Curry suggested that we go to Washington to see our congressman. The group agreed and we began to make plans to go. Our first step was to write a letter to the congressman requesting a meeting. This was done and we received a reply within 10 days. The reply letter stated that the congressman would be in his New Haven office the following week and would be pleased to meet a representative from our organization.

I was selected by the group to represent it. We drew up a list of requests to be presented to the congressman. It was decided that our focus would be on civil service jobs. The group admonished me to keep the focus on jobs.

The morning of the meeting came and I went down to the Federal Building to meet Congressman Geelan.

I walked into the office and was greeted by a female secretary who offered me a seat and a cup of coffee. She informed me that the congressman was in a meeting and would see me shortly.

After about a ten minute wait the secretary told me that the congressman would see me now.

Congressman Geelan was a slightly built man who stood about 5 feet 8 or 9 inches tall. He walked toward me with his hand extended and greeted me with some comment about knowing my family. He said that he knew my dad and my uncles Roland and Jack. He also added that he knew my mother's brothers Major and Billy. All of this happened before the secretary had announced who I was. To add a little icing to the cake he said that he was glad that I had returned from the Southwest Pacific unharmed.

I believe my mouth opened to say something but I don't remember saying anything until he said, "Now what can I do for you?"

Looking back to those few moments I realize that I was totally overwhelmed. I did say something about the fact that I was there about civil service jobs primarily post office jobs. He said that would be no problem, that he would personally speak to the Postmaster. I don't remember asking for anything else.

I do recall there being a pause and him saying "If that's all, thank you for coming in to see me." I said "Thank you" and started to leave the office. The congressman said, "What can I do for you?" I turned and said something to the effect that I wanted jobs for my veteran brothers. He said, "What can I do for you?" I repeated my earlier statement. With that he walked over and patted me on the shoulder and said "Good-bye."

Some years later I told this story to some friends who were savvy politicians and one of them asked if the congressman had delivered. I replied affirmatively but added that only three or four jobs had been obtained. I also noted that the congressman had been voted out of office. One of my political friends asked if my group had worked to help the congressman to be re-elected. I replied that we had not. Then my political friend said, "Charlie you made two mistakes. One was when you failed to tell the congressman what <u>you</u> wanted and the second was when you didn't work to help keep him in office. He went on to tell me how politicians view people like me. "People like you" he noted "can be problematic. Remember a person who can't think of anything that he wants for himself sure can't really want anything for anyone else."

He went on, "Further the second mistake was not setting your group up as a power base by coming out to support the congressman. Win, lose or draw you would have established yourselves as a force to be recognized."

Well, as I noted in my opening statement, I think my classmate was wrong when he thought I should have run for office.

An office seeker should have a clear picture of what he (she) wants for self. That picture must encompass a constituency. If that constituency is unitary, that is to say, only focuses on self, then there is a problem. If the picture includes a broad diversity of ideas which can be articulated then the office seeker is on the correct path and can represent his constituency with impunity.

I chose to play the role of gate keeper to ascertain that the office seekers had a clear picture of what and who they were promising to represent.

Family Values

Kay and I were talking not too long ago about the differences in the way we remember being disciplined by adults for our youthful misdoings. My wife Kay did not relate any instance in which she was physically disciplined by an adult. I, on the other hand, related a number of such incidents.

Kay was raised in a strong family environment in which Christian values played an essential role in her life. Though many people perceive this type of environment as being somewhat sterile, it was not by any means. Kay's early life was filled with the love that only a Christian family can provide.

I was raised in a Christian family environment. For a long time I was an only child. My parents attended church every Sunday during my early years. Sunday school played an important part in my life. Yet my life was filled with conflict. My mother and father fought on a regular basis. But somehow I was able to maintain many of the Christian values that both my parents wanted to instill in me. Of course they had help because others took an interest in my well being. There was a support system, a safety net.

Both Kay and I were raised with strong beliefs in the idea that there were consequences for misbehaving that were not pleasant. I, for example, learned that stealing was wrong and though it took awhile, I avoided the temptation.

At first I thought that getting caught stealing was the sin. I had tried it a few times and my mother used a hairbrush, a switch, a stick or whatever implement was handy to whip (not spank) my behind. Mother showed no mercy. Then her words which either proceeded or followed the corporal punishment hurt equally as much.

Her words still ring in my mind, "I don't care how poor we are I will not tolerate a thief in this house" or "God knows what you did and only He can forgive you." "You stole that candy from Axelrod's now you're going to take it back and face Mr. Axelrod and admit that you stole it." "I cannot believe that you would embarrass your family by stealing."

These statements and many more were spoken to me in my early years. I don't know why it took me so long to get the message that stealing was not an activity that would be condoned by my mother and father and God.

I don't have children of my own but I became a teacher and had the opportunity to be a part of many young people's lives. I became a part of the support system, a piece of the safety net. During my years as a classroom teacher and as a principal I often times wanted to emulate my mother but the law and public opinion placed some restraints on how far I could go. But there were times when a whack on the knuckles of a miscreant youngster, or a yardstick on the behind of a bully, or the uttering of some fear inducing words, were used. I am not certain how effective my actions were but I have had young men and women approach me on the street and say – "Thank you for what you did for me."

Though my mother has been gone for a long time I don't believe it's too late to say – "Thanks Mother for instilling those Christian values in me along with just a modicum of fear."

March 12, 2007

My wife and I were watching the Today Show and Ann Curry reported on the mugging of a woman 101 years old. The pictures that were shown were horrific in that the mugger brutally hit this frail woman repeatedly then punched her down. These pictures were captured on a surveillance camera.

Both of us were outraged at the activity and joined in the chorus of angry people who wanted this animal caught and punished.

As we discussed this terrible deed I recalled seeing a purse snatching take place on upper Broadway in New York.

The incident took place on a Saturday morning on Broadway near 110th Street. People were out shopping on this beautiful spring morning. The fruits and vegetables in the various markets were all polished and displayed outside under the awnings. The sidewalks had all been washed and swept.

Saturday morning shopping was sort of a ritual among many of the residents of the neighborhood. The chatter was infectious and there was a lot of banter between the pedestrians and the young people who worked at the various store fronts.

Suddenly there was a scream that overrode the chatter, the banter, and the sounds of traffic.

"Thief! Thief! Thief!" the screaming voice repeated over and over. The traffic along Broadway continued moving. The pedestrians kept moving. Suddenly a thin, no, a skinny young man burst through the pedestrians running as only a thief can run, pushing people aside.

Apparently no one was paying attention until the skinny young man, the one running as only a thief can run, either slipped or was tripped. I'm not sure! But he went down. When he hit the pavement he was suddenly set upon by at least twenty people who punched, kicked and otherwise abused the skinny body on the pavement.

There were two police officers standing at the corner of 110th and Broadway. I noticed that they glanced at the melee taking place on the pavement. After about five minutes they made their way to the crowd. They pushed people aside and started to pull the thief to his feet. He grabbed one of the policemen and clung to him. From my vantage point he was pretty beaten up.

The other policeman bent down and picked up a pocketbook. A lady ran up and claimed the pocketbook. But, the policemen held onto it and told the woman that she had to come to the precinct to identify the thief and claim her property.

Well, I started thinking about a mugging that took place a couple of days ago. I wish that what I saw a few years ago on Broadway could have happened to the lowlife that attacked that 101 year old lady. Though I don't advocate so called street justice I do believe a good old fashioned "street whipping'" at the proper time could act as a very positive deterrent to such senseless acts of violence.

With teenage buddies, Cousin Ray Pearle (front),
Russ McCabe (center) and Reggie McCabe (back right)
Circa 1938

With teenage buddies (back left to right), Leon Thomas,
Cal Stoner and Morris Simmons
Circa 1938

The Ravaloes
(Front) Ernie Towler, Russ McCabe, Milton Fitch
(Center) Bill McDonald, Howard Steadwell
(Back) Morris Simmons, Cal Stoner, Clayton Gilliam,
Me, George Musgrove, Winston Brown
(Missing) Leon Thomas
Circa 1938

My uncle, John Robinson
Circa 1931

*My uncle, John and aunt Katie Robinson at
sister Alyce's wedding, August 1960*

With Mrs. McCoy (Mrs. Moore's sister)
Sunny at age 2

At age 2 with childhood friend Ray
(Raymond Gershefski)

On pony
Age 2

My mother's brother
Major Robert Allen Jr.

My maternal great-grandmother
Sabina Carrelli Sanderson

My maternal grandfather
Major Robert Allen Sr.

My maternal grandmother
Catherine Sanderson Allen

With Isadore Wexler, Principal, Winchester School,
Dr. Estelle E. Feldman, Director of Pupil Services,
New Haven Department of Education and
Dr. Allen G. Hickerson, Chairman, Education Department,
New Haven State Teachers College (SCSU)
Circa 1955

With my students and colleague Frances McDonald and visitors
from business and industry to my classroom at Winchester School,
New Haven
Circa 1954

With Rose Marie McGilten, 7 and Stanley Wilson 5, at after school recreation program I initiated in New Haven Circa 1954

Diversity

I attended church service yesterday and must admit that I was moved by what took place and how it awakened my old brain to an earlier period in my life. The theme of yesterday's service was "Diversity."

The music, the Old and New Testament readings and the guest speaker's message all focused on "Diversity." The focus was not only on racial diversity but on the broader interpretation of diversity that includes thought, gender, political view, age and religion.

It has interested me over the past few years how much attention has been given to diversification of our societal structure. Much energy has been expended by various and sundry individuals and organizations to undo the social structures that have been intentionally constructed to separate people into various compartments such as race and class. Of course there are various other categories and sub-categories into which people have been compartmentalized.

The irony in this matter is the fact that when there was serious discussion underway in America about improving race relations – (For those who have a problem remembering – this was when America was perceived as being divided into two parts, one white, the other black) much effort was spent attempting to "integrate" the two parts.

Integration became the word "du jour". To integrate was to be politically correct. The nation worked at integrating schools, neighborhoods, social organizations and many other bastions of white society. Of course most of the energy was spent by middle and upper middle class white and black persons of all classes. Well, there was an exception – Black militants did not believe in being politically correct. They believed that integration was a step toward racial amalgamation; loss of racial identity and that meant the end of blacks as a viable political entity in the racial pattern that makes up American society.

The problem might have resolved itself if American society was in fact divided into two parts. But this was not to be. It soon became evident that American society was made up of many parts. There were racial groups that were not yet perceived as part of the general society.

Black activists were not ready to give up the fight for equal rights and recognition that African-Americans were equal to white people in every aspect. They felt that any disparities that existed were due to deprivation of education, adequate health care and the ravages of slavery. For this latter disparity they sought reparations.

With the push for reparations came a strong resistance from white society which claimed no responsibility for the acts of its forebearers. It was about this time that white society discovered the rich diversity of race and culture in the United States. It was also the time that immigration from Mexico became a problem and the national economy became somewhat unstable due to business and industry outsourcing work to other countries.

Diversity has now become the term "du Jour". It went way beyond the narrow term integration of blacks and whites. It encompassed new racial, ethnic and cultural groups. It was inclusive of the societies to which jobs and whole businesses were now a part. Above all it removed the onus of having to address the problems attendant to demands of reparations to one group (i.e. the progeny of slavery).

Maybe a focus on diversity will somehow remove the rancor of "integrating" two races. Maybe through diversity we will become as the black activists feared – amalgamated. Then the fight for integration will become moot, at least as far as race is concerned.

Racism (4/15/07)

Today a TV/radio comedian/commentator by the name of Don Imus has been taken to task for some inappropriate remarks he made. These remarks were considered to be both racist and sexist. I listened with interest since the castigation was emanating from a white male news commentator.

Prior to his commentary he had interviewed two prominent black civic leaders, both of whom had been unsuccessful candidates for president. Both men had a history of being outspoken critics of any white person, company or institution who spoke in derogatory terms about black persons or institutions. These two men might be called first responders. Some have called them opportunists.

The two black civic leaders did their job well. They called for the companies that hired Imus to fire him. They called upon the advertisers to withdraw their financial support from the Imus program. This was perceived as a good move.

I have some concerns about the apparent satisfaction with the above actions. By now as a reader of my essays you might have surmised that I have some philosophical differences with what might be considered the norm. So in keeping with that pattern I ask the following: If the behavior of Imus was so reprehensible so as to fire him, why didn't those who sought closing down Imus also call for the firing of those who sustained him for more than 20 years?

According to what I've read and heard, Imus has belittled, demeaned and in other ways dehumanized people of color, women, and any others that he and his team selected. He did this knowing full well that because he had the bully pulpit there would be no effective response.

So now an opportunity presents itself, an opportunity to not only slap the maggot but to get rid of the garbage upon which it feeds. If the two civic leaders (and others) are truly concerned about the mean spirited shenanigans of Imus, so called rappers, shock jocks, public purveyors of half truths and those who claim to espouse the causes of God, then they would call for national boycott of the corporate sponsors who have by their own avarice become the garbage upon which the maggots feed.

I suppose a person such as myself can afford to be critical of the heroic civic leaders who bravely lead from someplace behind the garbage. For some, this is a good place depending on the wind direction.

Yearbooks

My wife Kay asked me about my high school yearbook which she had never seen. I went up to the attic and found my high school and college yearbooks. I noticed that the pictures in the yearbooks looked remarkably similar though there was a ten year gap in time that the books were published. 1940 and 1950.

I graduated from high school in 1940 and from college in 1950. I was seventeen when I graduated from high school and twenty-seven from college.

Kay, my wife, who is much younger than I thought that I was handsome at age seventeen. My! How time has impacted such thoughts. People now describe me as distinguished I would guess that as one ages and develops grey hair (at my age white hair) how else can one be described?

Now I am the one who looks in the mirror each morning and the reflection tells the truth. The truth is – I'm still here sixty-seven years after that high school yearbook picture, and fifty-seven years after that college yearbook picture.

I think back to that period that I spent as a high school senior. I remember so vividly walking to school with my buddies and talking about going to college. There was no thought of how I was going to afford college. I just knew that I was going. No thought was given to how I was going to qualify for admission with marks in some subjects below average. I just knew I was going because my guidance counselor told me that I should be satisfied to get a "good job." She told me that my dad was a waiter and that was what I should aspire to.

She had no idea that two of my mother's brothers had attended college and that one of them was a practicing dentist. She had no idea that my mother had studied vocal music at a distinguished university. She had no idea that my desire to attend college had been nurtured by my family.

Now I must confess that I did not exhibit any outstanding academic qualities. I was quite distracted at that time by a number of non-academic concerns.

One of those concerns was that I was not living at home with my parents. My folks had legally separated while I was still in junior high school. I was living with our former landlords, Mr. and Mrs. Moore. He was a retired chef with the Pullman Company. These folks were sort of like surrogate parents.

Another of my concerns was my very strong interest in young women. I had an uncle who set an example for me. He was known as a ladies man and I wanted to emulate my uncle.

This leads me back to my wife Kay's description of my looks at age seventeen. According to my female relatives I could "get by" on my looks, and I tried. Needless to say this took a toll on my homework time.

I've come to the conclusion that yearbooks open many doors in the minds of folks like me.

Sometimes the doors that are opened reveal some hidden delights.

Reunions

High school reunions never excited me a great deal. I have lived most of my life in New Haven. Of course I spent some years in the army. Other than that I was never away for more than a few weeks or months.

All that I had heard about high school reunions seemed to focus on what people had done with their lives over the past ten, twenty, forty or so years. Well if you live in a community for many years you pretty well know what people have been doing.

Now, during this era, family reunions are the style. Everyone seems to be involved in developing plans or actually involved as a participant in a family reunion. Family reunions work when the family has been disbursed around the country or around the world.

Well, to get back to high school reunions, I decided to attend my fifty year reunion.

This came about due to a little pressure from a long time friend, Ernie. Ernie and I had lived in the same neighborhood and attended high school together. We also attended the same church.

One evening after a church meeting I told Ernie of a phone call that I had received from a member of the 50th reunion committee urging me to attend the reunion gathering. I commented that I didn't feel that I wanted to go since I had no ties to anyone in the class with few exceptions. Ernie said as only he could – "You should go." My response was one word – "Why?"

Ernie smiled and said – "Charlie I attended the 20th. 30th, and 40th. reunions and at each one several people asked about you." Now my interest was awakened. I remember saying, "Ernie, who would be asking about me? My life is open to the public. I've gotten calls from a number of people when my name appeared in the newspapers. I've gotten calls from my good friend Pat". Pat and I had been on the football team together and had been in touch over the years.

People reading this should understand that the class of 1940 graduated about 1,114 students. Fourteen of those were African-American. African-Americans comprised about 3.5% of the class.

The school had a long and distinguished history in its academic achievements. It also had a great athletic tradition. I did not have an outstanding high school career either academically or in athletics. You might say I was average.

Getting back to Ernie. He had a way of pressuring a person without really appearing to do so. He just said – "You should go Charlie!"

So I went.

The first person that I saw upon my arrival at the reunion was Ernie. He just nodded and winked his eye. I wasn't sure what the wink was about but entered the large meeting hall and was immediately surrounded by several of my "classmates". They all seemed to know my name. Of course I was wearing a name tag but these people seemed to really recognize me.

I didn't recognize anyone in that group. But I did a quick name tag read and began to respond calling names and acting as though I was addressing long lost friends.

One of the group took my elbow and guided me away. As we stood a few feet away he said, "I'm Leo." I glanced at his name tag and nodded affirmation. He then continued in a very soft voice to inform me that he and his buddies had been very jealous of me and my buddies because we were considered to be quite well off.

After the shock had passed I asked him why in the world he and his friends could ever have reached such a conclusion. He went on to tell me that it was because of the way we dressed and our general demeanor. Leo said that the fact that we wore tweed sports jackets, white buck shoes and oxford button-down collar shirts set us a step above.

I guess I shocked Leo when I let out a loud – "What the hell are you talking about." Then it dawned on me exactly what he was talking about. I was tempted to keep secret the source of Leo and company's chagrin. But, I decided to tell him.

During the time period that I attended this school many of the African-American community worked at Yale University. At that time Yale had many financially well off students. These students every now and then over spent their allowance and found themselves strapped for funds.

When such financial problems presented themselves the student solution was simple. Find Jack.

Now Jack was the proprietor of Jack's New and Used Clothes. Jack was always available to buy quality used clothes from the students. His purchases included Harris Tweed jackets, grey flannel pants, oxford shirts and on occasion white buck shoes. Jack also made friends with the African-American men who worked on campus as janitors or waiters. These men were also the source of clothing that was discarded by students. Jack would now and then purchase items of clothing from these men.

Jack was also known to contact his African-American friends to let them know when he had an item that might fit one of them or one of their kids.

My buddies and I were the kids of Jack's African – American friends. My dad used to say, "Those rich boys weren't too proud to sell their clothes and I wasn't too proud to buy them."

So, because my dad and his friends knew a good deal when it came up we kids dressed quite well. We also adopted a demeanor that fit the clothes. In fact we did act rather snobbish. Leo may have indeed had reason to be jealous.

I didn't tell Leo that my dad told me that some of the white men who worked on the Yale campus let it be known that neither they nor their kids would ever wear cast off clothing.

Well, reunions do have their reward. Thanks to Ernie and Leo.

Home Again

I woke up this morning at 6:10 A.M. and realized that I was thinking about Mr. Moore who was a great influence in my life.

As I have previously stated, Mr. and Mrs. Moore were the owners of the house where my family lived shortly after I was born.

Mother and Dad separated when I was ten years old. It was during the Great Depression and Dad had lost his job as a chauffeur. His job had taken him to New Jersey and he and Mother had drifted apart. That part of my life is a whole other story.

But getting back to Mr. Moore, the man who had a great influence on my life. At age fifteen I went to live with Mr. and Mrs. Moore. As a result of the separation of my parents I was to live with my father. My sister was to live with my mother. This was an order from a judge who in his infinite wisdom thought this was an ideal arrangement. Retrospectively, I'm not too sure.

Dad was still a young vigorous man. He was a handsome man and in today's vernacular a "chick magnet." He attracted some real fine looking women.

We lived in a small apartment above Doc Holly's drugstore. Dad worked as a waiter at one of the country clubs and part-time at one of the Yale clubs. He was away a good part of the day which left me on my own to get into mischief. And I did! I guess I too attracted a few chicks.

Dad and I got along quite well until one of his lady friends began to show interest in me. I won't go into details but Dad asked if I would like to go live with my mother who was living in New York. I opted to try it. So I went to New York during the summer. It was great! I met some great guys and we did a lot of things that city guys did.

Mother worked downtown and was away most of the day. I soon learned my way around the neighborhood and looked up my buddies daily. We walked everywhere. I learned that twenty blocks north and south was approximately one mile. Mother lived on 146th Street. so that the twenty-one block walk to 125th. Street was a piece of cake. As you read this you probably have figured out that there are many more stories to come from this period in my life.

Getting back to Mr. Moore. When I returned to New Haven in September Dad asked if I would like to live with Mr. and Mrs. Moore. I told him that I would really like this. The Moores were very special people to me and this was truly a wonderful gift.

Well, I moved into the Moore's home and was given the front bedroom. The room was large and bright. It was adjacent to the dining room. The dining room would later play a significant role in the lives of seven young men.

My first days at the Moore's were truly wonderful. Mr. Moore had not fully retired from the Pullman Company. As a result Mrs. Moore and I spent a great deal of time talking. It reminded me of when I was a little boy and she would talk to me about the things around us. She loved flowers particularly dahlias. She also had a vegetable garden.

Since it was September most of the vegetables had been picked. The dahlias were still flourishing along with a mass of sunflowers. The vegetable garden had several cabbage plants and a large number of turnips. There were still some tomatoes and the corn and onions were waiting to be harvested.

Mrs. Moore had a wide brimmed hat which she wore in the garden on sunny days. On this particular Saturday, Mrs. Moore asked me to go to the yard with her to harvest some of the vegetables. She donned her wide brimmed hat and we went to the yard. I awaited Mrs. Moore's instructions as to what to do. Her instructions were quite simple. "Pick your dinner."

Only God knows what precipitated that comment. But, I know what went on in my mind. I thought how really blessed I was to have found a truly loving home.

That evening Mr. Moore came home and the three of us sat down to a real tasty meal of cabbage cooked with bacon, sliced tomatoes and onions, corn on the cob, cornbread and iced tea.

Stories

Mr. Moore loved to tell stories about his youth growing up in Canada. He loved to tell about the doctor in Montreal who told him at age 21 that he wouldn't live until his twenty-third birthday if he continued his wild life style. Mr. Moore lived to be ninety-nine years old.

Mr. Moore used to tell of going into a bar and asking for a glass of wine which he used to rinse his mouth in preparation for a bottle of champagne. He told of waking up thirsty and having a shandygaff to assuage his thirst. He never drank anything stronger than tea in all the years that I knew him.

He lived during the era of the famous comedian Bert Williams. Now Bert Williams was probably the fountainhead of all modern African-American comedians. One of the stories that Mr. Moore used to tell was as follows: A gentleman of color is summoned to court as a witness in a murder trial. There were several other witnesses all of whom testified that they had heard one shot fired at the victim. The gentleman who is the subject of this story insisted that he had heard two shots. After lengthy interrogation, the judge finally intervened. He said, "Young man, everyone at the scene of the shooting heard one shot. How is it that you heard two?" The young man without hesitation replied, "Your honor, I heard the first shot when it passed me and I heard the second shot when I passed it."

This story was a classic Bert Williams. Mr. Moore had about ten recordings of Bert Williams performing the "Elder Eatmore Sermons." I wish that I had that set or recordings now. They were great.

Trust

Have you ever gotten drunk? I mean real, seriously drunk! Well I did and I'd like to share the experience with younger readers. I'm assuming that anyone who reads this is a younger reader.

I was sixteen and living in my wonderful home with my dear surrogate parents Willis and Mabel Moore. The group of young men with whom I associated were all two to three years older than me. Why they tolerated me is still a mystery. I believe that it was maybe because I was sort of a free spirit. I was not living with my parents. I had a lot of freedom because Mr. and Mrs. Moore trusted me. Yes, trust was a big factor during the era in which I grew up.

Today I guess my friends and I would be referred to as a posse or maybe a gang. I believe that the big difference, between then and now were the goals set by the youth of our era and the goals set by present day youth. During our era our goals were quite clear. We aspired to middle class standards. Our role models were not television characters nor were they movie stars; they were real people, people who were known to us; people who we saw each and every day. Our role models were mail carriers, soldiers, writers, club stewards, railway employees (Pullman porters, dining car workers, red caps) truck drivers and chefs. These were the men who we saw going about their daily tasks with purpose and pride. These were our fathers, uncles, older brothers and family friends. One should also recognize that among all of our role models there were those who were number writers and bootleggers.

These men were known as hustlers. There were also members of the clergy whom we looked up to as well. Within this whole population there were also wife beaters, pilferers, liars, and drunks.

We were raised in this environment and were nurtured by mothers, aunts and grandmothers all of whom were knowledgeable of the strengths and weaknesses of our role models. These women consistently would call to our attention how gentlemanly uncle so and so, or how neat and clean Mr. such and such was. They also were quick to caution us not to emulate the behavior of Tom, Dick or Harry. So the reader can quickly see that our group of young men lived in a protected environment. There was a concerted effort made by the woman in our lives to protect each of us so that we might grow to achieve a productive manhood. Speaking of manhood, I was not admitted to manhood until age thirteen that was the age at which I was allowed to wear long pants. This means that the era to which I refer was just three years into that most hallowed state of manhood.

A female friend of mine who lived in a nearby town invited me and three of my buddies to a birthday party. I was most happy to have been invited to this particular party because I knew that it meant many beautiful young ladies would be there. The young lady was the daughter of a well known clergyman. My mother had been a soloist several times at my friend's father's church.

The day of the party came and my friend Clayton was driving his dad's car. He picked me up and then the other guys. We rode the nine miles to the site of the party. On the way we stopped and one of the guys purchased a bottle of gin and a bottle of sloe gin. We all knew that alcohol was prohibited but we were sixteen, seventeen and eighteen years old. We were all good kids. We were all trustworthy. No one told us not to bring liquor to the party. We knew better.

It was decided prior to our arrival at the hall where the party was to be held that I would have the responsibility of hiding the bottles. I had been to the hall once before so it was assumed I knew the layout. We also knew that people would become suspicious if we left the hall to go out to the car. With two bottles hidden in my jacket pockets I went directly to the lavatory which was at the rear of the hall.

I entered the lavatory and went directly to the toilet bowl located the reservoir which was located above the toilet bowl. I stood on the toilet reached up and deposited the bottles in the tank. The water was very cold.

Upon my return to the hall I joined in the fun and dancing. I also told my friends where the booze was hidden. It was November, the hall was toasty warm. During the evening I made several visits to the lavatory as did my buddies (except Clayton). By eleven o'clock I began to feel woozy and headed to the car.

I remember Clayton telling me to get out of the car and go into the house. The ride from the party to my house is not in my memory bank. The trip upstairs to my room was like being on a ship on a stormy sea. I made it to my bed and flopped. I had to hold onto the bed because it was spinning around and tilting violently. Sometime during the early morning I threw up. I was violently sick and did not make it to the bathroom. But I had a hat and a wastebasket nearby which I filled to overflowing.

Sometime later in the day I was awakened by someone shaking me and calling my name. When I finally awoke and painfully focused on the person who was shaking me I was shocked to see my dad. My eyes focused on his face which was usually pleasant to gaze upon. The face that I saw was not pleasant. This face was an angry face and did not give me the usual feeling of warmth that I generally felt when I saw my dad. He had never raised his voice in anger at me – except once. My dad ordered me out of the bed and for the first time I got a whiff of what I had regurgitated. I also got a look at my bed which was soiled. I started to rise from the side of the bed and almost fell down. My dad held me up and walked me to the bathroom.

Once in the bathroom Dad started to fill the tub with water. I took off my soiled clothing (I still had on my party clothes) and stepped into the tub. It took a few seconds for me to realize that the tub was filled with cold water. I believed that it was too cold but my dad pushed me down into the tub. The shock of the cold water on my body cut off any sound coming forth from my mouth! After what seemed like an hour I stood up, grabbed a towel, and dried myself.

When I returned to my room; I found the shades raised and the windows up. My dad ordered me to take my hat and the wastebasket and empty them of the vomit I had placed therein. The smell was overwhelming. Dad further ordered me to pick up my clothes and to strip the bed. I had by this time; put on some fresh clothing. My stomach was still very upset. I sensed that my dad was restraining himself from hitting me and I therefore did not say anything.

When I finally got my room straightened up my dad ordered me to sit down and listen to what he had to say. My dad was a man of few words. He said that he was embarrassed that he had to be called to sober up his drunken son. It seems that Mrs. Moore had called me to come to breakfast and when I didn't answer, had peeked in my room and got a whiff of the vomit and the sight of the room that I had trashed. She wanted to come in to comfort me, but Mr. Moore vetoed that action and called my dad.

Dad made it quite clear that I had broken all the rules but most significantly I had broken a trust. He pointed out that when I went to live with the Moores I had promised that I would behave like a mature gentleman and would do nothing to embarrass either he or my mother and especially nothing to hurt or embarrass the Moores. Those were all people whom I dearly loved and I had broken a promise and a trust.

I was not directed to speak to the Moores. When I walked out of my room I heard them in the kitchen talking. I had to face them. I walked into the kitchen. There they were sitting at the table drinking tea. Neither of them looked at me. They stopped talking but continued to sip their tea. I waited a couple of moments and finally said – "I got drunk." They said nothing. I said – "I'm sorry". Mrs. Moore started to get up from her chair and Mr. Moore told her to sit down. He then asked – "So, you're sorry you got drunk?" My response was quick – ""Yes sir." He just nodded. It then dawned on me, Mr. Moore had given me an opportunity to be a man and I had blown it.

I walked over to where he was sitting, faced him and said, "Chief I'm so sorry that I broke your trust in me. Please forgive me!"

He stood and took my hand and shook it. He didn't say anything. He walked into the dining room and started to talk to my dad. Mrs. Moore stood and gave me a hug.

I cried.

Prom Preparation

In 1939 my buddies and I decided that we were going to attend the senior prom. I was not a member of the class of 1939 but my friends decided that I was going to attend.

I was the youngest member of the group but by no means the smallest. The guys liked to visit my house because they all thought Mr. Moore was really great. When he heard that I was planning to go to the prom he offered to help me get ready.

We had a club called the Ravaloes. The name came from the story of Silas Marner. In the book there was reference to the village of Ravaloe. We took our name from this book.

I invited the Ravaloes to meet at my house after getting an O.K. from Mr. and Mrs. Moore.

The club meeting at my house was unlike any of our others in our history. There were twelve of us in the club and Mr. Moore had set the dining room table (a large round table with two extra leaves).

He placed twelve chairs around the table. He told me that he was setting up the table to resemble the way boards of directors often set up their table. He had me make two large pitchers of lemonade. Mrs. Moore made a large pan of gingerbread to accompany ham sandwiches which Mr. Moore had prepared.

All of the Ravaloes arrived on time and needless to say were quite impressed with the setting for the meeting. It was quite a change from our usual meetings sitting around someone's living room or basement. Our meetings usually lasted about two hours (most of which was spent in pointless arguments abut nothing of real importance.) But this meeting was different. It was structured. We had an agenda which Mr. Moore helped develop.

Before we left the meeting we knew exactly what we needed to do to achieve our goal of successfully attending the prom. I felt very gratified in that Mr. Moore had helped us in such a positive way. He was not my dad but he gave me the kind of support that a dad needs to give to a son.

I was indeed rich. I had two dads and two mothers.

The Prom

The class of 1939 held its prom at the State Armory in New Haven in March (I don't remember the exact date). There were twelve of us who planned to attend with our dates. With few exceptions our dates came from outside New Haven. The young ladies that we invited to attend the prom were by far the most attractive in the state. We knew, because the year before, our club had run a popularity contest which involved girls (young women) in all the major cities in Connecticut.

Our popularity contest required the contestants to sell votes. Each vote sold for five cents. The contestants had one month to sell the votes. The winner would be determined by the total number of votes sold. Each young lady was given 20 books of 100 votes. There were 20 contestants representing ten towns. To make a long story short - We made money. But more importantly we met a number of new very attractive young ladies.

We went through the usual screening that the parents of young ladies put young gentlemen through. We all attended church. We were all in school and as far as the parents knew we didn't smoke, drink or curse.

As a result of the contest some of us met young ladies and invited them to the prom. Some of us already had out of town contacts.

Easter

As a young teenager I looked forward to Easter Sunday. Easter Sunday meant going to Easter sunrise services atop East Rock. Our church youth group (Allen Christian Endeavor) joined with youth groups from Immanuel Baptist, Dixwell Congregational and St. Luke's churches. We all had youth group leaders, usually divinity students from Yale Divinity School.

For the first couple of years we would meet at one of the churches at about 4:00 A.M. We would have cocoa, sandwiches and cookies and then start our walk to the base of East Rock.

Once we arrived at the base of East Rock we joined youth groups from other churches from around the city. We then began our ascent to the summit. Some of the more adventurous youth broke off from the main group and walked up a trail on the face of the rock. We used to call that trail the Giant Steps. I tried it one time and got frost bite in both hands. Once was enough.

The group usually arrived at the summit in time to assemble with other worshippers from around the area. There were prayers said and songs sung and then came the sunrise.

Easter 1944 was spent in New Guinea and I spent early Easter morning on a hilltop. There were prayers, there was singing and the sun rose. Our prayers were for an end to the war and protection from the enemy. We sang "Christ the Lord is Risen Today, Alleluia, Alleluia, Christ is Risen Indeed."

Easter is indeed a special day today in Bermuda, yesterday in New Guinea and day before yesterday in New Haven.

Shame

There are a number of things that take place during the course of your life that you'd rather not have to think about. The mean words that you spoke, that were intended to hurt; the shove or push that you gave to someone that you knew couldn't or wouldn't push back; the taking advantage of someone who is lacking the intellect to challenge you. Some of these incidents are best forgotten but they seem to linger in the deeper recesses of the mind.

I have at least one such incident that seems to consistently push itself forward in my mind.

When I was eighteen I like many in my generation was looking for employment. I wanted to attend college but didn't have enough money to pay tuition. There was another factor that had to be considered. I had not achieved good academic grades – also I was a C student. Not withstanding I sent for applications to several colleges in the South. I received one – Virginia State College in Ettrick, Virginia.

This application form is at the crux of my guilty recollection.

My buddies and I were visiting a club in New York. (It was legal to be in a club at that time if you were eighteen.) Part of the entertainment was a dancer who was about as pretty as any girl I had ever seen. I believe my buddies were equally impressed. This young woman appeared to be about my age.

I must admit I lusted for this lovely young woman and told my buddies that I was going to date her before we left

New York. My mother was living in New York at that time, but had no idea that I was in the city.

We (my buddies and I) had pooled our funds and rented a room at the Teresa Hotel. We hoped to score before we went back to New Haven. I was able to get the attention of the young woman and mouthed – "See me after the show." Well to my surprise, after the show the waiter tapped me on the shoulder and whispered that a young lady at the bar wished to speak to me. I told my buddies, and Russ handed me five dollars. (He was the designated banker for the trip. We always pooled our money when we hung out together.) I went over to the bar.

Sitting at the bar was the dancer. She was even prettier close up. I walked over to her and she held out her hand and said, "Tina". I introduced myself. Before I knew it I was telling her about my position as part owner of a club in Connecticut. Somehow or other I found myself offering her a job at my club. During our conversation I sensed that "Tina" was not too bright. I then told her that we (my buddies and I) would like to see her art in private. I told her that we had a room at the Teresa Hotel where we could view her act. She agreed on condition that she could bring a girlfriend. I agreed to this and I gave her the room number and the time.

I left her at the bar and rushed back to the table to tell my buddies. I did not tell them of my perception of Tina's intellect. We went back to the hotel and prepared for Tina's audition which was set for 2:00 A.M.

Tina arrived with her girlfriend and we began talking about "my" club. We finally got around to the audition. Tina stripped down to her underwear and began to gyrate without music, just to the panting of three horny teenagers. She danced about 15 minutes and then came over to me and asked how much I was going to pay her. Without pause I said $75.00 a night for two nights.

Her girlfriend called Tina aside and the two of them whispered for a few moments and then Tina asked me for a contract. I had no idea what a contract looked like but I did have my application for Virginia State in my jacket pocket. I trusted my instincts and pulled out the application which I flashed at Tina. I wrote on the front on the application $75.00 per night to be approved by John Doe. I handed her the piece of paper which she took and perused. She handed it back and said it was okay. I then told her I had to get John's approval and would send back the signed contract.

Tina and her girlfriend left the hotel at about 4:00 A.M. leaving three panting still horny teenagers. My buddies congratulated me for being a smooth operator and I in turn puffed up with pride.

It wasn't until a couple of years later that it struck me that I had done an evil thing. I had taken advantage of someone who didn't have the tools to fight back. Though I've done a few other things in my life this one keeps pushing to the front. I really regret having taken advantage of Tina.

Stealing Corn

My wife was driving along South Shore Road and we saw a cyclist standing on the seat of his bike picking loquats from a tree overhanging the road. I told my wife of an experience that I had during my teen years.

I was about sixteen years old and was a passenger in a car driven by one of my buddies. We had been to visit some girls in Suffield (CT). It was during late summer and about 7:30 P.M. We were passing a cornfield. The corn was tall and waving in the breeze.

The sight of a field of moving corn is sort of magnetic. It draws one's mind to a place of tranquility. It lulls one to a point of euphoria.

However the sight of a waving field of corn evoked a somewhat different response in our teenage minds. We seemed to collectively arrive at the same conclusion – Corn on the cob.

Morris stopped the car. We got out, ran into the field and began to pick ears of corn from the stalks. We each picked about six ears of corn. We returned to the car and put the corn in the trunk. We continued our trip to New Haven and discussed our foray into the field of corn. We also talked about how we would enjoy the succulent, fresh, sweet corn drenched with butter and sprinkled with salt.

Upon our arrival in New Haven we went to Russ' house. We retrieved the corn from the car's trunk and set about shucking the big, beautiful ears of corn. We admired the symmetry of each row of kernels.

The corn was placed in boiling water and we waited patiently for the corn to cook. Russ said his mom usually put a little sugar in the water, so we did that.

After about ten minutes we took the pot off the stove and went to the back porch. We poured the water from the pot to the ground. We each took an ear of corn, spread it with butter, sprinkled it with salt and took our first bite. The ears were at least ten inches long.

That first bite was not into the juicy sweet corn that we were used to eating. That first bite was into the most tasteless, mealy, tough corn that any of us had ever experienced.

We had stolen two dozen ears of feed corn. This corn had been planted to feed livestock.

Well maybe it did feed four jackasses.

Right Hand Man

My career as a classroom teacher was relatively short. I taught for twelve years in the elementary schools of New Haven, CT. Those twelve years were probably the best years of my professional life. It was during those years that I utilized the skills that I had learned while in college. More importantly I got to know some real great kids.

Reflecting back to that period in my life I also got to learn some new skills that would shape my future both professionally and socially.

My professional life has been shaped by people who took an interest in me at various stages of my life. But my focus in this piece is that period between 1948 and 1963.

I was a student at New Haven State Teachers College in 1948. I was also working part-time at two jobs. One job was as a bartender at a private men's club. The second job was as a kitchen helper at two of Yale's secret societies. At each of my part-time jobs I met people who would have an influence on my life.

One of the persons later became president of a university; another became mayor of New Haven and gained national recognition. The person who became a university president also had worked part-time while at Yale. He liked to tell people when we happened to be at meetings later in life that I was his right hand man. The reference was to our days as servers at Yale in the dining halls and secret societies.

It is strange how a person (such as me) perceives either the establishing of a philosophical base or the influencing of an established philosophical base by either other people or incidents. One's beliefs are generally based upon that person's exposure to various stimuli.

My early exposure to positive thinking males both in my family and in my community had a profound influence on me in determining the direction my future life would take.

Though I never truly aspired to become a top athlete my relationship to my dad and his brothers all of whom were top athletes guided me to explore my own capability to achieve some success in baseball, basketball, tennis and golf. My mother's brothers also contributed to my interests in sports. Two of her brothers were outstanding in many sports. They were also baseball and football players and one brother was also an ice hockey player, ran track and played basketball.

During my early years I was witness to the exploits of my uncles and listened with pride to the plaudits of their fans.

Though no one in my family pushed me to play any particular sport I always felt obligated to try to play in each area. I played baseball, football, and basketball. I ran track and tried hockey. I played tennis and still play golf. But I never learned to swim.

Part of the process of assimilating the positiveness of my uncles and dad's athletic exploits is the factor of not being forced to try to emulate any one of them. The exuberance and the seriousness with which they approached sports impacted my understanding and belief in how one utilized these skills in every day existence.

These observances served me well as a soldier in the military during World War II. I, like many young men of my generation, entered the service with very limited knowledge of what it was all about. What I did know was that our country was at war and I had been called to serve.

Maybe I'm overstating the limitations of my knowledge about what the military was all about. I had served several months as a volunteer in the Connecticut State Guard. (The State Guard was a replacement for the Connecticut National Guard which had been federalized in 1941). As a member of the State Guard I had learned about military law, military discipline and close-order drill. These elements alone gave me an advantage in my basic training.

This early training of course meant that I could engage the training with a confidence that very few recruits had. As a result I was made a corporal quite early in my training. This early promotion gave me increased confidence and incentive to want to advance even higher. It was a catalyst for utilizing those attributes endowed to me by my uncles.

I started this piece on writing about how various life experiences had affected my professional life. My military experience was indeed significant. That experience gave me the confidence to put forth my own ideas. I was also able to utilize the ideas of others so as to make a project successful without undermining the confidence of the originator of the idea. I have found this to be important in assuring a project's success. So often projects fail because the initiator of an idea is totally ignored and thus becomes alienated.

Without my early exposure to sports by my dad and uncles and my experience in the military, it is questionable whether I could have accomplished the success I experienced as a teacher or social activist. The degree of success may be questioned by some but on a comparative basis I did pretty well.

Isadore Wexler

Isadore Wexler's name will always be omnipresent in my mind. My first contact with Mr. Wexler, or Wex as I later in life called him, was when I was a fourth grade student.

Wex was a physical education teacher who visited Winchester School. I remember how diligently he worked to teach us how to perform the various gymnastic exercises. He was young, handsome and energetic and all the kids respected and admired him.

I lost track of Wex over the years and did not come into contact with him until 1949. I was interviewed by Wex, his wife Leonore, and Ed Harris for a job as a camp counselor. I was a senior in college at the time and expected to graduate the coming June (1950).

The interview was successful and I was hired to work as a counselor to a group of six and seven year olds. I was surprised at the amount of information the interviewers had about me. They had done their homework.

That summer I worked at the camp and also applied for a job as a classroom teacher. This began a long and rewarding friendship with Wex.

The advent of working at a top of the line day camp was very exciting for me. Just the summer before I had been assistant director of an overnight camp owned by the Dixwell Community House. I had been affiliated with the Q- House ever since I was six years old. My association covered my junior membership which cost ten cents. I was issued a membership card which I cherished. The card not only gave me access to the Q-House, it also made me a member of a very elite group. That group consisted of other boys and girls my age but also included boys and girls in junior high and high school. It also included many adults who not only were card holders but also worked as volunteers in the many programs the Q-House offered.

It was at the Q-House that I learned the importance of setting goals and working to achieve them. My parents were not able to send me away to camp during the summer months. But I did go to camp via a scholarship which required me to work as a cook's helper. I peeled potatoes, plucked chickens, swept, and washed pots and pans.

These early experiences prepared me to be a good camp counselor. Though I had gone to camp on a work scholarship I also participated in most camp programs.

My colleagues at Wex's camp were all college graduates and all were teachers. All of the male counselors (maybe with one or two exceptions) were former military having served in the army, navy, coast guard and marines. No one ever asked what I did while in service. The fact that we had all been selected to work at the camp and entrusted to work with children was a badge of acceptance and trust.

Working at the camp offered many unique opportunities to interact positively with kids and with people who were true peers. You rightfully ask – True peers? Yes. We were of the same age group, same education background, similar military experience. We had a sense of humor (collective) that allowed us to appreciate the bucket of steam, left handed screwdrivers jokes and pranks.

So it was in this setting that I began to professionalize my life. I began to feel comfortable utilizing my newly acquired college education. In fact in this environment I was expected to use those skills to make our campers' experiences memorable.

Dr. Martin Luther King Jr.

I spent about two hours this morning talking to and listening to a group of fourth graders. The group numbering about thirty-two came from the Mount St. Agnes School in Hamilton, Bermuda. They had been invited to the Bermuda National Gallery to view an animated film about the life of Dr. Martin Luther King and to meet someone who had met and talked to Dr. King and who had also participated in the March on Washington.

The class was predominantly Caucasian. There were maybe six students of color. Overall they were a real fine looking group of children.

My approach to this group was to establish my credibility with them. I first asked their permission to be seated while I talked to them. I explained that I knew how difficult it was to sit and look up at a person who was standing, especially if that person was over six feet tall. They gave me permission to sit. I then went on to tell them about how I got to meet Dr. King and how that meeting had affected my life.

Now one may get the idea that I'm about to launch into an essay on how to address a group of nine and ten year olds. This is not my intent. I wish to reflect on my brief contact with Dr. King.

I first met Dr. King when he was a Chubb Fellow at Yale University. My meeting with Dr. King was at the home of a Professor Bergin who was Master of Trumbull or Saybrook College.

The setting was the sitting room of Professor Bergin's apartment. Afternoon tea was hosted by Mrs. Bergin and the group was small, maybe 20-25 persons. It was here that I met Dr. King. My boss Isadore Wexler had arranged my invitation to the lecture and tea. He and Professor Bergin were friends and he sensed that Dr. King was slated for greatness. I was indeed fortunate to have been chosen.

During the course of the late afternoon tea Dr. King was told that Mr. Wexler and I were from the public school system and that we were a part of a new concept of public education. Dr. King expressed an interest and he and Mr. Wexler discussed this concept at some length. As a result Dr. King was invited to visit our school the next day.

Winchester Community School was abuzz when the announcement was made that Dr. King was going to visit the school that morning.

When Dr. King arrived we were notified by Professor Bergin that Dr. King would not be able to visit all of the classrooms since he would have only a half hour to spend at the school. We were told that his flight out of Bradley International had been moved up an hour.

Our auditorium held about 570 persons and would accommodate all of our students and staff. We announced to the school that we would meet in the auditorium at 9:00 A.M. to hear Dr. King speak.

The students, kindergartens through grade six filed into the auditorium and were seated when Dr. King arrived. Unlike previous assemblies when the students were together, there would be a lot of noise. Today there was a soft hum in the hall. One other thing was different. There were many parents in the hall. The word had gotten out that Dr. King was going to visit.

Dr. King arrived at approximately 9:00 A.M. We met him at the front entrance. We escorted him to the auditorium and walked to the front and up the stairs to the stage. My boss, the principal asked if I'd like to introduce Dr. King. I nodded my assent and proceeded to do so.

I don't recall my exact words except, "Boys and girls, Dr. Martin Luther King."

Dr. King began to talk to the assembled group in a soft voice. You could have heard a pin drop. He told the children what it meant to be non-violent. He told them how important it was for them to study hard and to behave. He told them of Mahatma Gandhi and told them of St. Matthew's admonition to turn the other cheek.

When he had completed his talk he said that he would answer questions if there were any.

One student, a fourth grader as I recall, stood and asked Dr. King if he was serious about turning the other cheek. Dr. King smiling told the student that he most certainly was. He then asked the student to come to the stage. He then proceeded to tell the student the Russian parable about the sparrow in the hand of the grandfather. This was the story in which the grandfather held a sparrow in his hands and gave his grandson a choice as to whether to free the bird or condemn it to death. This would come about depending upon the choice made by the boy.

Dr. King held out his clenched hands just as the grandfather might have done and told the student to select a hand and pointed out that he had a choice of freeing the bird or condemning it to death. The boy hesitated and then said, "I don't know which hand holds the bird." Dr. King replied, "I know. But you have a choice."

The youngster said if I pick the wrong hand the bird will die. Dr. King replied, "You have a choice." With this the boy asked if this meant that he had a choice of turning his cheek or hitting back. Dr. King smiled and said, "that's right and it takes a brave person to turn the other cheek.' He gave the boy a pat on his head and said, "I know that you are a brave young man."

I believe that student grew to six feet. His smile illuminated the auditorium and he literally glided to his seat.

The Lincoln Adventures

I don't know if anyone cares that I once owned a brand new Lincoln Continental automobile. Lincoln automobiles hold a special place in my heart. One might say that I was raised around Lincolns and Pierce Arrow limousines. My dad spent a few years employed as a chauffeur.

My dad had utmost confidence in Lincolns. To my recollection he drove a special made twelve cylinder Lincoln. His employer was a police commissioner which at that time was a very prestigious position. It also indicated that the person had money (i.e. rich).

The family lived on Gregory Street at that time. I believe that I was six or seven years old when Dad was a chauffeur. He had one day off each week and would bring one of the big cars home. I looked forward to this day because I was allowed to play in the car. It was huge. My friend Raymond and I used to play in the back of the car which was about the size of a room.

One day Dad told me to gather my friends and we would be going for a ride. Beside Raymond, there were four other boys and we all fit comfortably in the back of the car.

Now all of this is to establish my familiarity, love, and respect for a Lincoln automobile.

On this particular day my dad took my buddies and me for a ride. We all sat in the rear seat with the exception of me and Ray. There were two jump seats in the rear and I chose the one just behind the driver's seat. Ray selected the one on the other side.

We were soon on our way. Dad began the trip by driving around the neighborhood. There was no air conditioner and so all of the windows were rolled down. We hung out of the windows and shouted to the people on the street. It was really great fun especially when we traveled up Dixwell Avenue.

Dad then took us northbound up Dixwell Avenue. None of us (except Raymond) had ever been more than five or six blocks north of Gregory Street. This was indeed a new adventure. We were headed out of town. Out of town during this period in my life was a great adventure. A trip to any of the towns bordering New Haven was indeed a special event.

The car headed toward areas that none of us in the rear seat had ever seen. We followed the trolley car tracks past the junction of Dixwell and Shelton Avenue and continued north toward unknown territory. We saw houses and stores and open spaces. We saw railway tracks and my father told us that these were the tracks upon which the circus train traveled. A little later my father told us to look to the left and we saw a hillside with hundreds of trees – apple trees.

Dad turned the big Lincoln limo around and we headed back to New Haven. We had traveled about four miles. He slowed the car and made a left turn into a huge field. He stopped the car. He got out and I spotted three other kids and some grown-ups just standing and looking up. So I looked up as did my friends and we saw an airplane.

The airplane appeared to be very high in the sky. Then without any warning something fell from the plane. As we stared it became clear that it was a person falling through the air. We and all the others standing on the field stood with mouths agape watching the body hurtle through the sky.

Suddenly, sort of like magic, a white sheet opened about the falling body. It seemed that the white sheet was attached to the falling body. The body seemed to stop its rapid descent and just sort of hung in the sky for a few seconds. It then resumed its downward journey but at a much slower pace.

In what seemed like a real long time, the body, now identified as a real live person, hit the ground. The person hit the ground running and pulling the big white sheet toward him.

The person who had jumped from the plane was wearing a cap with chin straps. He also was wearing goggles. We all ran toward the man. He had stopped and was still gathering the sheet.

The man removed the leather helmet and goggles and unhooked the sheet which I later learned was called a parachute. As we approached the man he turned his back and pointed up to the sky and wonder of wonders there was the two winged airplane coming right at us. It seemed to be almost touching the ground. All of us instinctively ducked.

The plane zoomed by and then flew almost straight up. The plane turned right and then around and headed in our direction once more. But this time the wheels touched the ground and raised a dust cloud as it rolled to a stop some distance away.

We stood and gazed at the plane. It turned and slowly headed in our direction. The sound from the engine was quite loud and the dust cloud was huge. As the plane drew near the man who had parachuted from the plane motioned everyone in the small crowd to move back. Then the plane's engine seemed to get louder and then it stopped. There was silence. Then a person stood up in the space behind the pilot and jumped down from the plane.

The group that had been on the field prior to our arrival all ran toward the person who just emerged from the plane.

They hugged the person and seemed to be yelling at him. The person took off the helmet and we saw that it was a boy not much older than us. We learned that this day was his thirteenth birthday and his dad had given him an airplane ride as a present.

My buddies and I looked on in awe as the boy walked by with his father, family and friends.

My dad gathered us together and put us in the rear of the Lincoln limousine. After we got settled in my dad asked if we had enjoyed ourselves. We all responded positively as the car moved back toward the avenue.

That trip has stayed vividly etched in my mind and with it the fact that we rode in a special made Lincoln. For some reason that fact has popped to the forefront of my mind every now and then.

One of those now and then times occurred in 1963. I had been appointed principal of an elementary school. Believe it or not, the school was the Abraham Lincoln Elementary School. The school sat in the center of a middle class neighborhood which was in the midst of a transition from a predominantly white neighborhood to one that was rapidly becoming black.

One day while walking through the playground I overheard some boys talking. One was describing a beautiful car he had just seen. It seemed as though one of the local well known gamblers had driven by in a brand new white Cadillac. The boy described the car in detail. I wondered how he could have seen so much in what had been a fleeting look. One of the other kids said he too had seen the car and that it had in fact stopped for a few minutes outside the playground fence.

I listened with interest and heard the oo's and ah's of the boys' audience. Then one of the boys said something to the effect that a person had to be a hustler to buy a car like that. There was a chorus of "Yeah."

This conversation stuck in my mind for several weeks. Then I heard that the gambler had just opened a poolroom just a few blocks from the school and that some of my older students had been seen going into the establishment during lunch hour. (Kids used to go home for lunch).

I knew the law did not permit minors to frequent a poolroom to play pool. But this place sold popcorn, sodas and ice-cream. Some of my pupils' parents voiced their concern and asked that I do something to stop the kids from going into the establishment.

A visit to the establishment proved to be quite enlightening. The owner agreed that having young kids hanging around was not good for business. He agreed to barring the kids from his establishment during lunch time. He went on to point out that the kids needed some kind of recreation program that would keep them close to school. I told him how the kids were making him a hero because of his new Cadillac. He laughed and told me to go out and buy a Cadillac and I'd become a hero to the kids.

I went home that evening and informed my wife that I wanted to buy a new car. We had a 1958 Mercury. She agreed and thus I became the owner of a new car – a Lincoln. Though I could not take the kids at Lincoln School for a ride in the new car I let them get in and examine it. They oo'd and ah'd about the handsome dashboard and the maroon leather seats. They oo'd and ah'd about the size of the car.

But of greater interest to me was the comment I heard from one of my kids that I'd overheard on the playground say, "Mr. T's got the baddest car in the neighborhood."

As I said earlier, the reader probably could care less that I owned a Lincoln. But my dad, the man who introduced me to Lincoln automobiles drove me up the avenue to Hamden in my new Lincoln with me sitting in the rear.

If You Don't Know – Ask!

Unquestionably man is influenced in his thinking by the sum total of his experiences. The sum total of a man's experiences can amount to a total beyond comprehension. But even with an infinite number of experiences to call on there is a tendency to fall back on those few experiences with which one feels comfortable. It's sort of like putting on a pair of comfortable shoes when taking a walk. The shoes may be comfortable but may be run over and have holes in the inner sole that cause the feet to blister and become sore. A new pair of walking shoes on the other hand provides support and a new unrealized comfort.

How does this relate to man's treatment of his fellow man? Over the years I've noted that people select their associates based upon the level of comfort he/she feels in a given situation.

Several years ago I was asked to serve on the board of a prestigious philanthropic organization. I happily agreed to accept the invitation and was installed as a board member. The board consisted of three women and six men. When I attended my first board meeting I was greeted warmly and made to feel quite comfortable. I already knew two of the women and had met two of the men previously. Of course they knew a great deal about me. I was a retired public school administrator and was presently working at a small community college. I had been recommended by the mayor. What I didn't know was the mayor had been asked to consider recommending a Latino. The retiring board president, whom

I had known for a number of years, had confided in me that he had asked the mayor to appoint an African American to replace him on the board. He felt that the board needed to maintain a philosophical balance which he thought I would provide.

My previous experience with the board had been as an applicant for financial support for an organization whose board I chaired. This experience proved to be of value to me since the application process required me to come into contact with the program staff of the foundation as well as the executive director. What I lacked was knowledge of the inner workings of the organization. This I would have to learn.

The sum total of my experiences proved to work well for me as a new board member. I knew from past experience that one of the greatest errors I could make would be to try to B.S. my way. I believe my second meeting helped me establish a persona that would carry me through the seven years of my appointment.

The agenda indicated that the board would be receiving a report regarding our investment portfolio. When the finance committee started to give the report I noted that two of the board members showed signs of restlessness. They fidgeted with their papers and they moved about in their chairs. This was unusual behavior on their part since at the previous meeting and the early part of this meeting these two had appeared to be totally focused on every agenda item.

As I listened to the report it became clear that the finance chairman was giving a report that contained no new material. The information was new to me, but evidently it had been heard by the other board members before. To be quite honest I did not fully comprehend everything that I heard. However, one thing struck me. It appeared that the finance committee was reporting that the largest proportion of our portfolio was invested in a relatively conservative fund and the small proportion in a more aggressive high interest bearing fund. I simply asked the finance chairman "Why?"

A look of disbelief came over the chairman's face and he responded that I evidently didn't comprehend the intricacies of high finance. He didn't say it in exactly those terms. This opened the door for one of the two restless board members. He asked the chairperson if as a banker he had lost interest in making a profit in his investment. The question came from a bank president and the man who urged me to ask questions.

Now I can go on about this episode but I want the reader to understand that what took place in the foregoing incident was an example of how one's thinking and actions are in fact influenced by the sum total of their experiences. First and foremost I would not have taken the comment of the finance committee chairman without a sharp comeback. Past experience taught me to maintain my composure, especially if losing your composure could have long lasting impact on any other action that might be taken. It was obvious to me that the chairperson was not accustomed to be questioned by anyone he perceived as being below his station.

Yes, our actions are influenced by the sum total of our experiences.

Today

Today I entered into my thirty-ninth month of my second marriage. God has blessed me with beautiful gifts – love, happiness and a wonderful wife. But that is not what I want to write about at this time.

Somewhere in my earlier writings I stated that my earliest mentor, Mr. Willis Moore, told me that one day I would grow up to be President of the United States. Well, I didn't. But I worked to achieve at the highest levels of my abilities and as previously stated – I did pretty good.

Sometime in 1964 or 1965 I believe that someone told another young black child that he would grow up to be President.

Now I know that this is a stretch but I'd like to believe that that young child's name was Barack Obama. I'd like to believe that somehow that message got implanted in the mind of this child and that he worked throughout his young life to achieve this goal because he grew to believe in its possibility.

I have lived to see what I believe will become America's finest days. Though I never carried around a sign saying,"I'm going to be President someday," I did in my sub-conscience mind always work toward achieving the ultimate success. I wanted the best not so much for myself but for those I served and those who were close to me. I was told by those with whom I worked that my biggest weakness was not wanting for myself. This was not true. I always wanted something for myself. I've wanted happiness. I wanted to assure that my home would be safe. I wanted to know that children would have opportunities to grow up educated and be able to live without fear of war, poverty, or loss of freedom. I wanted to live in a world where there was hope and where one could look for the promises that only a democratic society can put forth. This is what was implanted in my mind very early in life. This is what I hope has been implanted in the mind of Barack Obama.

Certainly I and all other reasonable people understand the realities of life. One reality is that dreams often turn into nightmares and hope often turns to despair. But, without dreams and without hope people stop caring. They tend to give up on themselves, and care little for others. As a result people tend to be less than civil to others. They find themselves confronting others and are subject to be persuaded toward major confrontations such as gang violence or even to war.

How is this relevant to what is taking place at this time in America?

America has been involved in a war since 2001. We became involved because we had become attacked by people whose dreams had turned to nightmares and whose hope had turned to despair. This by no means is meant to imply they are excused from their perfidy. They did a terrible thing for which there is no excuse.

The point that must be emphasized is that they were persuaded by others that there was no hope and that dreaming was futile.

This concept is important to we who are believers in democracy. We must maintain a strong and abiding belief that hope exists and that dreams will come true.

Barack Obama embodies the concept that as Americans we must believe there is hope and that our dreams can and will lead us to a better world.

Yes, our collective world can become very much like my present world in which I have been blessed by God, have found happiness, love and a wonderful wife.

Epilogue

I have been writing over the past few years attempting to put on paper some of the thoughts that pass through an eighty plus year old mind.

One of the things that I discovered is that putting one's thoughts, one's ideas on paper can be difficult if one attempts to put order to what comes to one's mind in random order.

As one who has been trained to research and to seek primary sources this has truly been an interesting exercise.

When doing research for a study one must keep in mind what the study is intended to prove or disprove. In this instance I became the primary source. The writing(s) may prove or disprove the fact that an eighty plus year old can relate the past to the present.

I chuckle when I find myself relating incidents from my youth and then realize that there is only one other of my boyhood buddies still alive.

That buddy, Russ, called me a couple of weeks ago to inquire about my health. We exchanged health information. We talked about joint replacements, cancer, sight and hearing problems and our golf games!

Russ calls me Turkey when he talks golf. I believe he is a seven or eight handicap player and despite severe problems with arthritis he still gets to the course.

Now why did Russ enter the scene at this time? Was this a random thought? Or, was this a sub-conscious effort of my octogenarian mind to bring some order to what might seem to be mindless ramblings. I'm not quite sure. But what I do know is that regardless of my protestations that thoughts and ideas come to me in random order, the key word is "order".

Keeping this in mind – my thoughts as I wrote about my birth came when one of my mother's friends commented about my slightly bowed legs. She said that my legs were "pleasure bent." Well that comment stayed in the family archives for many years. How did that impact upon my writing about my birth?

Well, in my family – both sides (Mom's side and Dad's side) revered its men. My uncles were highly regarded. That is, if they were blood related. Those who married into the family were accepted but not as warmly as the brothers.

Boy children were and still are looked upon with favor. The fact that I was born on a kitchen table surrounded by women had been a standing joke among my uncles, aunts and friends of the family.

My writing has employed some dialogue. This, I'm sure raises the question "Did he/she really say that?" My answer to that query is, "Well, not exactly." Or "To the best of my memory – that's what was said."

Then one must wonder what really happened between my mother and father? If you read the story about my father's early days in New Haven you will understand that he was a country boy. He was farm born and spent the first twelve years of his life in the country. His father (my paternal grandfather) worked at a private school. I don't know what he did there but he recognized how important it was for his boys to be exposed to book learning. I do know that my grandfather was a knowledgeable horseman. I also know that he was very strict and was known on occasion to hit my grandmother.

Well, my dad whom I loved dearly never became a scholar but he was unquestionably one of the brightest men I've ever known. He was well read. He understood higher mathematics. He enjoyed the arts. He was an excellent athlete. But unhappily much like his father he did hit my mother.

My mother was a city girl, the daughter of a strict father and a mother who died quite young. Mother was the middle girl in a family of seven living brothers and sisters. She was gifted with a beautiful contralto voice and she was skilled in other art forms. Mother was a spirited woman who would never give up or give in to an opponent.

I believe it was the strength of both these individuals that led them to divorce. They literally competed against each other. Dad was a popular man in the neighborhood and especially at church. Mother was equally popular. Her beautiful voice was known throughout the community. She performed in concerts at several mainline churches and was often asked to do concerts in private homes.

Finances were a problem for Mother and Dad. Mother's concerts did not bring in any money. She would get a "thank" offering at some churches and an envelope from some of the "patrons" of the arts. The envelopes contained money, usually about ten dollars.

Both Mother and Dad worked. Mom worked as a cook, maid, baby-sitter, elderly caregiver and general housekeeper. Dad worked as a porter in a department store, a waiter, a chauffeur, professional baseball player, a brick maker, a houseman.

They filled all of these positions at some time in their early years of marriage. In retrospect they had a rough time. But, they were in love.

Things had gone fairly well in the mid and late 1920's. Then came the 1930's. And with that came the depression. They lost what little savings they had when their bank closed its doors. Jobs were scarce and help from any source was hard to come by.

Mother's voice provided some relief when she won a contest sponsored by the Atwater-Kent Company. As a result she was offered an opportunity to attend the Yale School of Music to study under a Professor Pease.

Somehow, and this I am not certain how, Mother's voice came to the attention of Miss Eva Jessey, a renowned choral director in New York City. This led to an offer to join Miss Jessey's choir. This caused some strain between my parents. In addition Mother also received an offer to teach music at a small school in South Carolina. This offer included an offer for my father to become the head groundkeeper at the same school. Needless to say the strain became greater.

Mother accepted the offer from Miss Jessey and began to sing with Miss Jessey's group. This move was not looked upon favorably by my father. I believe Dad saw this as a threat to his ability to take care of his family. Though my mother had worked at various jobs in New Haven and augmented my father's earnings with the income from these jobs, Dad could accept this because it was an accepted pattern in New Haven. But to go out of town to earn money – this was not acceptable.

To my knowledge mother did not physically move to New York. She joined Miss Jessey's group known as the "Original Dixie Jubilee Singers" as a soloist.

It was about this time that Mother formed a singing group of her own in New Haven. The group consisted of teenagers, male and female most of whom were members of church choirs. They became known as the F.C.T. Glee Club. The initials represented a well known singer of that era, one Florence Cole Talbot.

Most of the forgoing took place between 1925 and 1930. This was a very dynamic period for the Twymans.

It was during this period that Dad took a job with the McGraw family and moved to Madison, New Jersey. As pointed out earlier, Mother was spending time singing with Miss Eva Jessey and directing her own choral group. The group got an endorsement from Miss Jessey when she came to New Haven as guest director of the F.C.T. Glee Club.

I could continue writing about this period in our family's history. It is an important period because it shaped the direction life went for us in later years. It impacted on Mother and Dad's lives as they sought new lives without each other. And it certainly had a serious impact on my life and that of my sister.

My sister who was born in 1931 spent most of her early years with my mother. She spent those early years living with Mother and with some of Mother's friends when she was traveling. The friends with whom Alyce lived were very much like family and have remained so over the years.

I, on the other hand, spent time with my father and mother until given my independence at about age fifteen. I grew up real fast but not haphazardly. There were other people in my life such as Mr. and Mrs. Moore and my Uncle John and Aunt Katie and my Uncle Chick (whom I looked up to more or less as a big brother). But how could I have survived my boyhood without my dear cousin Amelia, my big sister. There were so many God driven interventions that I am hard put to take credit for my continued existence on planet Earth.

Without question, at least in my mind and heart, my sister and I have been truly blessed by God. Both our parents, despite their own problems never forgot to seek divine guidance and I truly believe that right up to this day their prayers guide us through the daily maze of life.

How else does one explain the narrow escapes that I experienced in my early years? How else does one explain the timely interventions at very critical periods in my life? The Moores became surrogate parents during the most vulnerable years of my life. My cousin Amelia, my protector, my confidant, was always there when I felt that the world, my world had abandoned me. But of greater importance was the fact that Amelia never over many decades ever forgot Mother's wish that she (Amelia) would complete college. She did. At age 83 she graduated from Central Connecticut University with a Bachelor's degree.

Yes, we were blessed each day of our lives and we learned how to live our lives, one day at a time."

Author's Note

I received word today (May 28, 2009) that my good friend of seventy years passed away at age 88. Russ was indeed a true friend and will be sorely missed. C.R.T.